CAMBRIDGE LIBRARY COLLECTION

Books of enduring scholarly value

Religion

For centuries, scripture and theology were the focus of prodigious amounts of scholarship and publishing, dominated in the English-speaking world by the work of Protestant Christians. Enlightenment philosophy and science, anthropology, ethnology and the colonial experience all brought new perspectives, lively debates and heated controversies to the study of religion and its role in the world, many of which continue to this day. This series explores the editing and interpretation of religious texts, the history of religious ideas and institutions, and not least the encounter between religion and science.

Origin of the Four Gospels

The pioneering textual scholar of the New Testament, Constantin von Tischendorf (1815–74), discovered and transcribed early manuscripts, notably the *Codex Sinaiticus*, his acquisition of which provoked long-lasting controversies. The original German edition of this book appeared in 1865, and sold 2,000 copies in three weeks; this English translation (1868) was based on the improved and expanded fourth German edition (1866). In it, Tischendorf applies his enormous knowledge of early Christian literature and the oldest Latin, Greek and Syriac gospel manuscripts to the question of the date of the canonical gospel texts, which, he argues, had been established by the end of the first century. Parts of the book are highly polemical, with Tischendorf referring to 'the Tübingen fantasy-builder and the Parisian caricaturist' in his attempt to refute contemporary theories about the person of Jesus. Nevertheless his translator engagingly describes him as a 'great and genial' scholar.

T0382549

Cambridge University Press has long been a pioneer in the reissuing of out-of-print titles from its own backlist, producing digital reprints of books that are still sought after by scholars and students but could not be reprinted economically using traditional technology. The Cambridge Library Collection extends this activity to a wider range of books which are still of importance to researchers and professionals, either for the source material they contain, or as landmarks in the history of their academic discipline.

Drawing from the world-renowned collections in the Cambridge University Library, and guided by the advice of experts in each subject area, Cambridge University Press is using state-of-the-art scanning machines in its own Printing House to capture the content of each book selected for inclusion. The files are processed to give a consistently clear, crisp image, and the books finished to the high quality standard for which the Press is recognised around the world. The latest print-on-demand technology ensures that the books will remain available indefinitely, and that orders for single or multiple copies can quickly be supplied.

The Cambridge Library Collection brings back to life books of enduring scholarly value (including out-of-copyright works originally issued by other publishers) across a wide range of disciplines in the humanities and social sciences and in science and technology.

Origin of the Four Gospels

CONSTANTIN VON TISCHENDORF
TRANSLATED BY WILLIAM L. GAGE

CAMBRIDGE UNIVERSITY PRESS

Cambridge, New York, Melbourne, Madrid, Cape Town,
Singapore, São Paolo, Delhi, Tokyo, Mexico City

Published in the United States of America by Cambridge University Press, New York

www.cambridge.org
Information on this title: www.cambridge.org/9781108043335

© in this compilation Cambridge University Press 2012

This edition first published 1868
This digitally printed version 2012

ISBN 978-1-108-04333-5 Paperback

This book reproduces the text of the original edition. The content and language reflect
the beliefs, practices and terminology of their time, and have not been updated.

Cambridge University Press wishes to make clear that the book, unless originally published
by Cambridge, is not being republished by, in association or collaboration with, or
with the endorsement or approval of, the original publisher or its successors in title.

ORIGIN

OF THE

FOUR GOSPELS.

BY
CONSTANTINE TISCHENDORF,
PROFESSOR OF THEOLOGY IN THE UNIVERSITY OF LEIPZIG.

TRANSLATED, UNDER THE AUTHOR'S SANCTION, BY
WILLIAM L. GAGE.

FROM THE FOURTH GERMAN EDITION,
REVISED AND GREATLY ENLARGED.

———◆———

LONDON:
JACKSON, WALFORD, & HODDER.
1868.

TRANSLATOR'S PREFACE.

———◦◇◦———

IT was a pleasant, sunny morning in May of last year, when I called at the modest house in Leipzig where the world-renowned Professor Tischendorf makes his home. It lies in a quiet, pleasant part of the city, away from its narrow streets, with their tall, grim, gaunt, gray buildings, some of them centuries old, away from the quaint churches, the castellated and fantastic Rath Haus, or City Hall, as we should call it, away from the places which Bach, and Mendelssohn, and Goethe, and Dr. Faustus used to frequent, and in the new and cheerful streets of the New Town. For Leipzig grows like an American city; its ancient limits no longer hold it in, but it is shooting away into the country on all sides, and turning the battle-field where Napoleon received his first great shock, into densely-built streets and squares. One would almost think that a paleographist like Tischendorf, a man whose life-work is the exhuming of lost and buried manuscripts and the making out of their contents, would choose for his home one of those old, weather-beaten, gaunt houses in the heart of the city; but when I saw the man, I could detect at a glance that it was not his nature to choose anything less free, pleasant, and cheery than those suburban streets, and their modern, sunny houses.

I did not venture to call upon this eminent man for the mere gratification of a natural curiosity, but for the purpose of ascertaining one or two facts which I needed for a note to Ritter's work on the Holy Land, which I was then editing and translating. As Ritter had been a near and valued friend of Tischendorf, it was a matter of great satisfaction to the latter that an American had proposed to give to the people of England and the United States a version of the works of that great and excellent man; and no welcome could be more cordial than Tischendorf extended. He is by no means the old, smoke-dried, bad-mannered, garrulous, ill-dressed, and offensively dirty man, who often answers in Germany to the title of Professor. On the contrary, Tischendorf is a man looking young and florid, though probably hard upon-sixty. I have seen many a man of forty whose face is more worn, and whose air is older, than that of this greatest of German scholars. Nor has he at all that shyness which a life in the study is almost sure to engender; he is free, open, genial, and has the manner of a gentleman who has traveled largely, and who is thoroughly familiar with society.

And if there is more than a tinge of vanity in his talk, if he does not weary of speaking of his own works, his own exploits, his own hopes and purposes and successes, we only feel that he can not praise himself more than the world is glad to praise him, and that all the eulogies which he passes upon himself are no more hearty than those which all the great scholars of the age have lavished upon him.

Tischendorf, like all really great men, is as approachable as a child, and is not obliged to confine his conversation to learned subjects. He does not speak English at all, but will give his English or American visitor the choice of five languages, — Greek, Latin, Italian, French, and German. In all of these he is at home, speaking the first four not in any stiff, pedantic way, but with grace and fluency. Yet he loves best his mother tongue, of course. In talking, his countenance lights up pleasantly, his style becomes sprightly, his action vivacious, he jumps up, runs across the room to fetch a book or document or curiosity, enters into his guest's affairs, speaks warmly of friends, and evidently enjoys with great zest his foreign reputation. Of two Americans he spoke with great warmth, — Prof. H. B. Smith of New York, and Prof. Day of New Haven. His relations with the great English scholars and divines are very intimate; and archbishops and deans and civil dignitaries of the highest rank are proud to enjoy the friendship of this great and genial German scholar.

Tischendorf gave me with his own lips the account, which in its printed form * is so well known, of his discovery of the ancient Sinaitic Bible. He told me of his three separate journeys to the convent at the foot of Mount Sinai in search of ancient manuscripts; of the bringing to light, at his first visit, of large fragments of the Bible as well as of valuable apocryphal documents; of his discovery in 1853, at his second visit, of only eleven additional lines from the book of Genesis; of the obstacles put in his way, the great liberality of the Russian government, the help afforded him by eminent princes, and the success which finally attended him, when, in the autumn of 1859, he was able to return from Cairo to St. Petersburg and lay the original manuscript of the Sinaitic Bible in the hands of the Emperor of Russia. It is one of the oldest written documents extant; dating back to the fourth century, about the time of the first Christian Emperor. No wonder that the night on which Tischendorf made this great discovery he was unable to sleep for joy, and danced in his room for very excitement.

Have any of my readers ever read Freytag's masterly romance entitled "The Lost Manuscript"?

---

* Given in the Massachusetts Sabbath School Society's recent publication of Tischendorf's little work for popular reading, " When were our Gospels written ? "

It seems to me that he has embodied in this work, which is one of the finest products of German genius, very much of the feeling which such men as Tischendorf experience in pursuing such investigations, and in coming to such results as this. But more momentous by far in its relations to the human race is the search for an ancient Bible than that for a lost Tacitus; the one the record of a nation's decline and ruin, the other the promise of a world's restoration!

During our interview, Prof. Tischendorf told me that he was then re-writing his work "When were our Gospels written?" making it a book for scholars instead of for popular readers, and enlarging it to three times its original size. He believed that both works were needed, in England and America no less than in Germany, and suggested to me to undertake the translation of the larger work. I promised to do so at my earliest leisure, and the result is now before the public. The name of the work 1 have ventured to change. In the German it bears the same title with the smaller sketch, "When were our Gospels written?" but fearing lest some should suppose that the two books are almost identical, merely different issues of the same work, it has seemed no violence to give the treatise the name, "Origin of the Four Gospels." The learned author has not succeeded in throwing his materials together in a way to attract hasty readers; his style is in this work rather heavy, hard, and disjointed; but great, invaluable facts are there; and there is no lack of a clear, well-poised, thoroughly guarded critical judgment, sound faith, and earnest purpose. If our Christian public at large have reason to be grateful for the publication of the little work of Tischendorf, our clergymen, theological students, and professors have no less cause to thank the great Leipzig scholar for furnishing them with this armory of bright, keen weapons to be employed in the overthrow of unbelief.

AUTHOR'S PREFACE.

———oo:⚫:oo———

WHEN in January, 1865, I set my hand to the task of preparing a work which should solve for the satisfaction of cultivated readers no less than of thorough scholars the question of the genuineness of our Gospels, — a question which stands related in the closest manner to the great topic of the present age, the Life of Jesus, — I was fully aware that those theologians who have for some time brought the scourge of their skeptical and unbelieving theories upon the field of New-Testament scholarship would take great offense at my work, and express themselves strongly against it. For who does not know that these men have long forgotten how to subject their prejudices to the results of conscientious investigation? Equally well-known is it that they are accustomed to regard nothing as having scholarly and scientific value unless it proceeds from their own circle. On my part, however, I felt it to be my duty to take up arms against this organized movement to convert theological science into so-

phistry, and give powerful support to the anti-
Christian spirit of our time; to meet it with the
results of rigid inquiry, and with the earnestness
of convictions which have matured from a lifetime
consecrated faithfully to Christian learning. It
seemed to be only in this way that I could advance
the sacred interests which I had at heart, and throw
light upon the questions which are vitally connected with belief in the Lord.

Did I expect to escape contradiction and the
anger of opponents? By no means. Others might
hesitate about committing themselves absolutely
to a service in behalf of the interests of truth, fearing to encounter the sharp thrusts which might be
directed against them; but I believed that I ought
to and must cherish no such fear, and solaced myself
with the thought that it would be a hard matter if
what I might suffer from the calumny of enemies
were not offset by the approbation of those who
believe in the purity of my intentions and the up-
rightness of my aim. I have not been disappointed
in this. The displeasure of my opponents has been
manifested in a shameless manner. But, on the
other hand, there has not been wanting the satisfaction of seeing my little book received in many
quarters with the warmest acceptance and heartiest
recognition, as well out of Germany as in it. In
France, Holland, England, Russia, and America,
translations have appeared; even an Italian one
was made at Rome. Yet opposition has at no sin-

gle moment failed to display its real character; the
weapons of lying, persecution, and calumny have
been brought to bear against me; and in so doing,
the blind zeal which has been displayed has at
times suffered the grossest ignorance to peep out.

Two men in particular have undertaken the task
of assailing my work with the weapons mentioned
above,— Dr. Hilgenfeld, of Jena, and Dr. Volkmar,
of Zurich. The first has devoted to this task an
article in the Review which he edits, heading it,
" Constantine Tischendorf as Defensor Fidei." As
examples of the disingenuous statements with
which he figures [strotzt], I adduce the following.
Although in my work my main task was with the
canon of the four Gospels; although I in no place
undertook to put the whole New-Testament canon
on the same footing, as, indeed, no thorough scholar
can· do; and although I do not speak specifically
of the whole canon, and merely put together as of
equal canonicity the four Gospels, the Pauline
Epistles, the first of John, and the first of Peter,
yet Hilgenfeld writes, p. 330: " The cheering result
which issues from this illustration of the subject is
the fact that the four Gospels, and even the *whole
canon* of the New Testament, can be assigned to
the close of the first century." Page 333: " Than
the presupposition that the close of the New-Testament canon falls at the end of the first century,
nothing is more incompatible." Page 336: " The
modern apologist, who puts a full and fair ending

of the New-Testament canon at the close of the
first century." Is this legerdemain, or a purposed
misleading of readers? It is, it must be, one of the
two. Naturally, he shuns quoting a single passage
of my work in support of the charge which he
brings against me.[1]

Page 333, note 2, Hilgenfeld, in commenting on
Euseb. Hist. Eccl. iii. 392, and alluding to Papias,
thus writes: "That the line of presbyters is opened
here by the apostles, can only be more than doubtful with a critic like Tischendorf." But would any
reader suspect from this that I was following the
express declaration of Eusebius, to whom we are
indebted for almost all our knowledge of Papias's
book, and to whose silence the negative school
itself is indebted for its powerful evidence against
John? And that the "Defensor Fidei" is here in
accord with the two heroes of the negative school
— Strauss and Renan — has not the third hero of
that school ignored this, or sought to whitewash it
over?

On page 337, Hilgenfeld writes: "The 'honorable weapons' on which Tischendorf prides himself
are, for that matter, made very doubtful even in
the homilies of Clemens Romanus." On this, he
proceeds to quote my words [in the first edition of
this book]: "It is of unabated interest that the alleged and acutely argued cropping out of John's
Gospel in this celebrated record of the Jewish-

---

[1] See notes in Appendix.

Christian tendency, based on the recent discovery
by Dressel, at Rome, of the closing portion of the
document, where there is an undoubted use of
John's story of the man whose blindness was healed,
— though it may be that the genial habit of skepticism will yield to no array of truth, — has entirely
fallen out of sight." On this, he remarks: " As I,
to whose critical investigations into the Gospels of
Justin a note at this point refers, do not wish to
hold Dr. Tischendorf to be a base calumniator, I
must conclude that he has taken a twelve-years'
slumber over the matter with which he is dealing.
Dressel's complete edition of Clemens's Homilies,
published in 1853, is for Tischendorf a book only
'just out.' Then he rubs his eyes, and simply
comes to the same conclusion that I came to fif-
teen years ago, before the conclusion of the Homilies was brought to light." To this I answer, that
my allusion to Hilgenfeld was coupled with the
expression " acutely argued," and that it was expressly stated that Hilgenfeld's words dated from
1850 ; and when I had occasion to speak of Dressel's work as " new," I appended the date, 1853.
Still some trace of his base calumniation must remain. And Hilgenfeld draws my own words,
" Though it may be that the genial habit of skepticism will yield to no array of truth," down upon
his own head. A glance shows that he is entitled
to the full application of it ; and one may not hear
of the " genial habit of skepticism " without seeing

that Dr. Hilgenfeld is alluded to. He acts as if he did not know that it is Dr. Volkmar who has so weakened his confession of a use of John's Gospel by the Clementines that the doubts respecting the authenticity of this Gospel remain undisturbed; and he writes: "But Tischendorf, although an honorable man in everything else, has in this instance been buried, with his critical knowledge, in the deepest slumber." Everywhere Hilgenfeld acts as if he believed that all that he advances must be contested by me: I did not purpose to take him for the subject of my book: he comes, as all can see, only under consideration so far as he follows in the direction which I oppose. Does he leave this direction at any point, and under any circumstances, he begins to cry out about "dishonor," "going to sleep," "Spanish knight-errantry," and the like, as in page 336, where says, "In him (Justin) I have long recognized the use of the three first Gospels, and even the possibility of an acquaintance with the fourth. This puts Tischendorf in the attitude of spurring his Rosinante, Don Quixote-like, against windmills as imagined giants, in his zeal to show the use of the four Gospels by these apologists." The zeal of the Spanish knight lies in the following forcible words: "That Justin repeats our Matthew in many passages is undeniable; that he knows and follows Mark and Luke, is in several places extremely probable."[2] Then a page and a half are devoted to a discussion of the effort which has been made to discredit this universally accredited result: as much more follows respecting the use of John, neither exactly answering to Hilgenfeld's views about fighting against windmills. Looking back at his loose statements, specimens of which have here been given, and more familiar with the discovery of his dishonesty, the same pitiable "Theologus quem terrestres certe superi . . . extra ordinem theologicum arcuerunt" writes in his "N. T. extra canonem receptum," "Ceterum Tischendorfii argumenta qualia omnino sint iam diiudicavi et huius viri subdolam in impugnandis adversariis rationem palam detexi." In the same work he boldly continues the flow of his dishonest effusions, writing on page 69, "Tischendorfium in famoso libello." . . . Page 44: "Calumniatoris partes agere, quasi negaremus Matth. evang. h. l. laudari nemo non videt." But what is on that page 44 to which he refers? Not a word respecting him; I only transcribed verbally what Volkmar wrote, where he prefaced his invectives against myself and others with the applause which he had received from Hilgenfeld and Strauss: "quod Ed. mea Esdræ Prophetæ; . . . omnibus qui hucusque de ea re ex Ed. mea iudicarunt persuasit, etiam Hilgenfeldio; . . . et Straussio. . . . Reussium satis pigebit." Is not this to wear without shame the liar's brazen brow?

But Dr. Volkmar has surpassed even Hilgenfeld in the use of these weapons. I had occasion to show in my book, by a number of examples, that a

great many trickeries had been employed for the
purpose of discrediting the evidence borne by the
second century to our Gospels. This evidence was
in part put aside, where it could be, by bringing
forward the testimony of lost writings; sometimes
the witnesses were made more modern than they
really were, and transformed from a decisive epoch
to one without significance, so far as the matter
under discussion is affected, while sometimes they
were charged with ignorance or deceit: here the
writings which gave evidence were regarded as
not genuine, or at any rate as interpolated so far as
to invalidate their testimony; while there the senti-
ments of ancient writers have all their pith taken
out by falsification and perversion. All this is effected by Volkmar with a skill that is unparalleled,
so far as my modest knowledge enables me to
judge. I ought not to refrain from giving some
instances of his ways of proceeding. In respect to
Herakleon, he writes, page 28: "Tischendorf states,
'This man was reckoned by Origen as contemporaneous with Valentine, which is confirmed by Epiphanius.' Yes, good God;* but if this is made out,
why waste another word upon it?" On page 130:
"Far from belonging to the earlier disciples of Valentine, he is one of the very last distinguished heads
of that Gnosticism, and one who would recommend it
to the Church: c. 190–195 on Luke, and c. 200–220

---

* A familiar oath used by German divines, ladies, and other persons,
and only less common than the hourly-repeated "Lord Jesus." TRANS.

on John." Now, on what does this assertion rest? First: "Origen only declares that Herakleon was accounted to be the friend of Valentine;" page 23. Second: "He was the chief opponent of the school of Valentine, unknown even to Irenæus;" page 210. Third: "This is confirmed by Epiphanius because διαδέχεται, in his language, only refers to the fact that the Half-Valentinians are followed in chap. 41 by the founder of Marcionitism in this, my Pana-rion of all heresies." But with all this, he has sought in vain to falsify history. Following the lead of Dr. Lipsius,[3] whose heresiological investi-gations Volkmar boasts that he has only continued with the greatest satisfaction to himself, he over-looks the passage in Irenæus, Book ii. ch. 4 (not alluded to [4] in the index indeed), where Herakleon and Ptolemy are distinctly mentioned as well-known personages. Having made this unfortunate oversight, he advances confidently to weaken the force of γνώριμος in Origen, to explain the διαδέχεται of Epiphanius in a joking fashion, and, lastly, to unearth in the ζητείτωσαν of Hippolytus a contempo-rary of Hippolytus between 200 and 220. Celsus encountered a similar fate. Respecting him, Volk-mar writes, page 80 : "Of Celsus's work, it is noto-rious that it manifested acquaintance not only with the canonical, but with the apocryphal Gospels, and more particularly with that of John." "It is quite another matter to determine the epoch of Celsus." "Celsus wrote his book about the middle

2

of the second century." "Does not Origen say, at
the close of his work, 8: 76, that this Celsus announced that he was intending to put forth another
writing of positive character, and that we must
wait to see whether he should accomplish his purpose? Does not this look as if he were a contemporary of Origen's? . . . What Baur has incontesta-
bly demonstrated, that the New Platonist opponent
of Origen was contemporaneous with him, is not
simply ignored by this Tischendorf, the appealer
to the ignorant multitude; it is absolutely unknown
to him." But the argument brought forward by
Volkmar rests on nothing less than a falsification
of the words of Origen; yet such a step could only
be taken by a scholar of his rare attainments, who
had neglected to read what Origen says expressly
with regard to Celsus, that "he had long been
dead." In both cases, therefore, in that of Celsus
as well as in that of Herakleon, there must be a
choice in the means of cure; at any rate, to those
which have been applied there must also be joined
the excision of the passage in Irenæus and Origen.
And is it not possible that the same Old Catholic
critic (found out by Ritschl) who had partly in-
vented and partly interpolated Ignatius's letters
and those bearing his name, and who at the same
time tricked out the Epistle of Polycarp with passages from Ignatius and Ignatius's Epistles, may
have had his hand in this matter as well?

That which personally touches me in these out-

pourings of theological bitterness is of very little
consequence compared with two other elements of
the document under consideration, — the frivolous
tone of its scientific pretensions and the treachery
to the church which it displays. For my own
part, I can only hold it as an honor to thoroughly
displease such men; and that my work has not entirely failed in reaching its mark, is proved to me
in no more effective way than by the calumnious
assaults which are made upon it; and so far as they
have tried to blacken over what I have done, I
freely pardon them, so far as roughness and want
of understanding are concerned: there would be a
valid token that I had failed in what I proposed were
I not the target for the unthankfulness of mockers.
But for the falseness which treads church and
knowledge alike under foot; for that hypocritical
frivolousness, which degrades the church into a
mere seminary for the propagation of untruth, and
elevates pure figments of the brain to the rank of
apostolical inheritances, I have nothing but a cry
of pain and of horror.

Only a few words regarding the new edition of
my work. The first edition, published in March,
1865, was followed in May by the second; the third
aimed at a greater popularizing of the subject, and
was accompanied by an historical sketch of my
travels and researches.[5] It now seems advisable
to add many details to that edition, and to make
an effort to make the work more complete and

valuable.   To do this, I have more than doubled
the amount of matter.   Of course it has been my
wish, in doing this, not to injure the work, so far
as its tone is suited to meet the wants of the general world of culture, although it is hard to produce
a book for this class, and at the same time to adapt
it to the wants of special sudents.   I must beg the
reader's indulgence, should I be found at times to
have given one body of readers undue advantage
over another.   I have written nothing which I am
not prepared fully to defend.   And may the blessing of God not be wanting to my little work in
its new form.

TISCHENDORF.

Leipzig, July 1, 1866.

CONTENTS.

——o——

21

ORIGIN OF THE FOUR GOSPELS.

HE life of Jesus has become the center of the religious controversies which agitate our age. The importance of this fact is great. At its foundation lies the confession that Christianity is not grounded so much on the doctrines of Him from whom it receives its name as upon his person. Every acceptation of the word Christianity which is antagonistic to this confession, disowns the real character of the term, and rests on a misconception. The person of Jesus is the corner-stone on which the church bases its foundations; to it the doctrine of Jesus and of his disciples always and with the utmost distinctness points; with the person of Jesus Christianity stands or falls. To rob this person of his greatness, —

of that greatness which the entire church ascribes to him under the name Son of God, —
and yet to think to retain the Christian faith
and the Christian church, is a futile attempt, a
vain mockery. Even the morality which some
might hope to rescue from the general ship-
wreck of faith is weakened by the unavoidable
and remorseless contradictions which arise ;
for if the morality is sound, it must be a good
tree growing from a diseased root. The life of
Jesus is the most momentous of all questions
which the church has to encounter, — the one
which is decisive whether it shall or shall not
live.

Whence do we derive our knowledge of the
life of Jesus ? Almost exclusively from our
four Gospels, in which the divine person of Jesus, the center of the Christian belief, and the
main object too of all attacks upon it, is pre-
sented in essentially the same light as in the
Epistles of Paul, unquestionably the oldest of
all the apostolical documents. All else that
we know of him is confined to a few expressions and acts, and, with unimportant excep-

tions, is in direct connection with, and dependence on, the Gospels. By far the most of
these sources are to be found in apocryphal,
i. e. not genuine, untrustworthy fragments, not
bearing the true names of their authors, and
aiming with more or less skill to supplement
and complete the gospel narrative ; others,
partly of Jewish and partly of heathen origin,
avow at the very outset the intention of assailing the Gospels. Finally, we possess in two
classic writers of the first and the two following centuries, Tacitus and Pliny, a few inci-
dental expressions which have a lasting interest : the first[6] testifying that Christ, the founder
of the religion which had gained so strong a
hold even in Nero's time, had been punished
with death by the procurator Pontius Pilate
during the reign of Tiberius ; while Pliny asserts[7] in a communication to Trajan that the
Christians, already a numerous body in Bithy-
nia, were in the habit of singing songs of
praise to Christ as to a God.[8] Our Gospels
therefore, if not the only authorities relative
to the life of Jesus, are by all odds the most

important ones, and the only direct sources
that are in existence. If then the life of Jesus is only made known to us by the Gospels,
if we are directed to these books for the solution of all our questions about the birth, the
activities, the conversation, character, and for-
tunes of Jesus, we have of course no less
weighty an inquiry before us than this, Whence
spring our Gospels? For upon the origin of
these books hinge their trustworthiness and
all their value.

So much depending upon this first step, very
many are the investigations which have been
made in these modern times into the origin of
the Gospels. It has been a question with what
justice the names of those prominent members
of the twelve, Matthew and John, and the
names of the helpers and followers, Mark and
Luke, have been assigned to the four Gospels.
Just so far as the authorship of these documents has been admitted as due to those revered men, the Gospels have been accepted as
authentic and trustworthy records of the life
of the Lord. Their names have been regarded

as a satisfactory guaranty that, in the writings
with which they were coupled, truth only could
be sought, that in them truth only was wished,
and that in them truth was authentically recorded. There is indeed another way of test-
ing the reliability of the Gospels. After the
rise of the rationalizing or rationalistic spirit,
and when the attempt was made to set the
reason of man above everything which had
previously borne the name of Divine Revelation, hands were laid at once on the biblical
miracles, and it was claimed that they must be
explained by the light of the imperfect culture
of that time, and the incorrect appreciation of
the Old Testament. Out of this grew the theory of accommodation, as it was called, which
asserted that Jesus made his words chime in
with the expectations of his age, and that he
gave himself out to be a more important per-
sonage than he really was. This theory of the
rise of the Gospels has culminated in the piece
of botchwork which issued from the Paris press
in 1863. The author of that book, not troub-
ling himself with any speculations respecting

the share which the apostles may have had in
delineating the gospel portraits, but following
his own self-imposed theories about miracles
and revelation, has displayed boundless reck-
lessness and given way to the most unbridled
phantasies respecting the gospel history, cari-
caturing both it and its hero. He has written
a book which has much more the character of
a shameless calumny of Jesus than of an honest investigation into his career. Can we apply the term historical inquiry to an attempt
to show[9] that John wrote the fourth Gospel
out of a spirit of self-love, not without jeal-
ousy of Peter,[10] and full of hatred to Judas
Iscariot?[11] Can we dignify by so high a term
as scientific investigation such a theory as his
respecting the cause of the sympathy felt for
Jesus by the wife of Pilate, that she saw the
" gentle Galilean," the " fine-looking young
man," from a window of the palace that looked
out on the temple-court, and that in consequence the thought that his blood was to be
spilled rested like a mountain load upon her
soul?[12] To cite one or two more examples of his

mode of dealing with the Gospels, what shall
we say of his manner of treating the raising of
Lazarus, where he endeavors to show that Jesus, whose role was becoming more and more
difficult every day, practiced an involuntary
piece of deception upon the people and the cred-
ulous sisters of Lazarus ? His theory is that
the latter, while still sick, caused himself to be
laid out for burial, and deposited in the fam-
ily vault ; that Jesus, wishing to see his friend
once more, caused the tomb to be opened, and
on seeing Lazarus come forth was himself led
to believe that the dead man had come to life
again, — the power of resuscitating him, mean-
while, being ascribed by the witnesses to the
wonderful gifts of Jesus.[13] Or what shall we say
of a theory of the conflict in Gethsemane,[14]
which seeks to throw light on the Saviour's grief
by such words as these : " Perhaps his thoughts
were running back to the clear springs of Galilee where he had often found refreshment, to the
vine-stock and the fig-tree beneath whose shade
he had rested, to the young maidens who it may
be had responded to his love. Did he curse

his hard fate, which denied him all the old joys
of his life ?   Did he lament his high call, and
weep, a sacrifice on the altar of his own greatness, that he had not continued to be a simple
Nazarene artisan ? " [15]   What shall we think of
the supposition that the dreary landscape of
Judæa — with Jerusalem, the sacred center
of the Jewish faith and worship — drove the
thoughts of the Galilean to the luxuriance of
his own country's hills, and added to his grief ? [16]
What shall we say of his exclamation, that
if a better understanding of Christianity is to
prevail among men, and the apocryphal shrines
which now claim veneration are to be super-
seded by authentic ones, the temple, the great
church for all Christians, is to be built upon
the hill of Nazareth, — the soil beneath which
are sleeping the carpenter Joseph and thousands of Nazarenes ? [17]   What shall we say to the
crudest of all Renan's vagaries, the investing
with the crown of immortality and the glitter-
ing halo of a saint the head of that Jew dying
on the cross, at the outset a mere kindly poeti-
cal enthusiast, and at last an idolizing fanatic,

involved irretrievably with the dominant party, and rushing willingly into the arms of death ?[18]

Surely it requires no further citations to justify the expression of a condemnation of Renan's book: these few instances are sufficient to put the reader in possession of materials adequate to enable him to judge of the character of the work. That, in spite of its frivolous pretenses to science, in spite of its fantastic caricatures of history, it has found such favor and endorsement in Germany, only shows how widely are diffused, even in Germany, the lack of sound criticism, and of acquaintance with biblical history, as well as the depraved taste of an age which is sunk in unbelief.

In this matter, German science and scholarship have subjected themselves to a severe reproach. Not only is the prevalent rationalism, which places our common human reason above a divine revelation, and so sets aside the supernatural claims of the Gospels, a product of this French book, but German zeal is aroused, as well, to supply what is lacking of scientific accuracy in Renan's work, and to make his results more trustworthy. And so we have one of the frightful spectacles of our time, — French levity and German learning reaching brotherly hands to each other over the fresh grave of the Saviour. Unbelief, it would seem, gives even more strength than belief.

In those quarters where regard is paid to historical authority, one of the points brought into the foreground in the attacks upon the authenticity of the Gospels, is the lack of early evidence that they were in existence at the opening of the Christian era. Nor can any one deny that this objection, if it can be maintained, is entitled to much weight. If it is as late as the year 150, or still later, that we receive the first tidings about John's Gospel, who would not find it hard to believe that it was written by the beloved disciple of the Lord a half century before? If there is not in our possession evidence in support of the other Gospels dating from that time, or from the years just preceding it, who can deny that it does not raise doubts respecting their authenticity? It is true, we must take into account the paucity of the liter-

ature which comes down to us from the earlier
epoch of the church; and besides, many a good
book might have been written without verbally
incorporating or directly using our Gospels;
especially at a time when those who had been
eye-witnesses had not been long dead; when
the life of the churches was directly sustained
by the spirit of the Gospels; and when the written letter had not begun to be dominant over
the living evangel. If these considerations
diminish the importance which might be attached to the absence of biblical quotations in
the primitive Christian literature, yet it is
clear, on the other hand, that if such quotations are really to be found there, the manifest
acquaintance which they might show that men
had with the Gospels in the first half of the second century must be of the greatest weight in
establishing their age, their apostolical origin,
and their genuineness. And therefore it is a
sacred duty that those who would subject the
authenticity of our Gospels to a thorough scrutiny, should make one of their chief duties a
most careful investigation into the most ancient

3

sources of testimony respecting the existence
and the recognized credibility of the records of
Jesus' life.

It seems to me that this duty has been by no
means faithfully enough met for the first three
so-called synoptical Gospels, and still less for
that of John, whose want of authenticity has
been inscribed in flaming letters upon the ban-
ners of the negative school. The writer of
these lines imposes upon himself the task of
trying to throw some light upon the authority
of the evangelical documents, although in preparing the work not for special students, but
cultivated Christians generally, it may not be
possible to enter so exhaustively into the subject
as under other circumstances might be desir-
able.

We can make as our starting-point the unquestioned fact that in the last decades of the
second century our four Gospels were known
and acknowledged in all portions of the church.
Irenæus, from 177 on, Bishop of Lyons, where
the first Christian church of Gaul was established, wrote a great work in the last decades

of the second century, directed at the earliest
heresies, the Gnostic, and on every page made
use of the Gospels, providing himself from them
with materials to overthrow a system which
was threatening to destroy the doctrines of the
church. The number of passages where he
has recourse to the Gospels is about four hundred, and about eighty of these contain quotations from John. From the closing decade of
the second century on, the able and learned
Tertullian lived and labored at Carthage, in
Africa, and in his numerous writings there
exist hundreds of citations from the text of the
Gospels, which he made use of as his most decisive authorities. The same is true of Clemens,
the celebrated teacher in the school of catechumens at Alexandria, about the end of the second century. Nor must I fail to allude to a
catalogue, generally known by the name of its
discoverer, the Italian scholar, Muratori, of all
the books which were regarded as canonical in
the very earliest times. This work was probably prepared at Rome, and shortly after the
time of the Roman bishop Pius, i. e. some-

where between 160 and 170. In this catalogue of the books thus reckoned as comprising the New Testament, the four Gospels are at the head.[19] It is true, the first few lines which relate to Matthew and Mark have been lost; but, at the close of the still extant words respecting the latter, the Gospel of Luke is spoken of as the third, and that of John as the fourth; enabling us to see that even in the very earliest days the order was followed with which we are so familiar.

I have thus summoned witnesses from Gaul, from proconsular Africa (the present Algiers), from Alexandria, and from Rome. Two others can be cited fitly here, although one of them goes back to a remoter date: I mean the two oldest translations from the Greek text used by the apostles themselves. One of these is the Syriac version, and bears the name Peshito; the other is the Latin version, known under the title Itala: both of them give the four Gospels the first place. The canonical acceptance of all four must unquestionably have been general, as we see that they were transferred openly, and

as a whole, into the language of the newly-con-
verted Christians, the Latins and Syrians.
The Syriac translation, which takes us to the
neighborhood of the Euphrates, is almost universally assigned to the end of the second cen
tury; and, although positive proofs are wanting
in support of this date, yet we are not without
good grounds for accepting it. The Latin version, on the contrary, had begun to gain general recognition even before the end of the second century; for both Tertullian, in his quotations from Irenæus, and the Latin translator of
Irenæus's great work against heresy, writing
about the end of the second century, make use
of the text of the Itala. This, of course, im-
plies that the Latin translation was made some
years before the close of the second century. I
shall have occasion subsequently to allude again
to the striking fact that it was necessary to
translate the Gospels into Latin and Syriac as
early as the second half of the second century,
and that the number of documents was limited
to the four with which we are now familiar.

Looking a little more closely into the testi-

mony of the two great Fathers, Irenæus and
Tertullian, we have to ask, Can their evidence
be so limited in its application as to only prove
that the four Gospels were fully accepted in their
day? Irenæus not merely invests these documents with entire authority in the citations
which he makes to overthrow the Gnostic heretics; it even appears in his work that the Gospels, or rather, to use his own expression, the
fourfoldness of the Gospel, has been conformed
to the analogy of the four quarters of the globe,
the four chief winds, the four faces of the cher-
ubim. He asserts that the four Gospels are the
four pillars on which the church rests as it cov-
ers the whole earth, and in this number four
he recognizes a special token of the Creator's
wisdom.[20] Is such a representation compatible
with the fact that at the time of Irenæus the
four Gospels first began to be accepted? or
that an attempt was then being made to append
a fourth and newer one to the three older ones
then current? Is it not much more credible
that the acceptance of all the four was then of
so long standing and so thoroughly complete,

that the Bishop of Lyons could allude to the
fourfoldness of the Gospel as a thing universally
recognized, and in consequence of this very recognition speak of it as a thing which harmonizes with great and unchanging cosmical relations? Irenæus died in the second year after
the close of the second century, but in his youth
he had sat at the feet of the venerable Polycarp, who had been a disciple of John the evangelist, and had been acquainted with many eye-
witnesses of Jesus' life. In mentioning this
fact Irenæus[21] alludes very tenderly to the statement of his revered teacher Polycarp, that all
that he had heard from the lips of John and
other disciples of Jesus coincided fully with the
written account. Yet let us hear his own words
as given in a letter to Florinus: "I saw you
while I was yet a youth in Lower Asia with
Polycarp, when you were living in scenes of
princely splendor, and when you were striving
to gain the approval of Polycarp. What took
place then is fresher in my memory than what
has occurred more recently. What we took in
in our youth grows up as it were with us, and

is incorporated in us.   And so I can even now
bring back to mind just the place where the
good Polycarp used to sit when he talked to us,
how he looked as he came in and as he went
out, how he lived, how he used to speak to the
people, how he used to allude to his intercourse
with John and repeat the words of others who
had seen the Lord, how he used to recount
what he had heard from their own lips about
the miracles and the teachings of the Lord, —
and all in full accordance with the written narrative." [22]

Thus writes Irenæus respecting his intercourse with Polycarp and respecting the communications of Polycarp.   The date of the young
Irenæus's intercourse with the aged saint must
be set approximately at about the year 150.   Irenæus died in 202, according to old accounts a
martyr, while Polycarp perished at the stake in
165, " after having," to use his own expression,
" served the Lord eighty-six years."   And is it
to be believed that Irenæus never heard from
his teacher, whose communications respecting
John he expressly refers to, one word regarding

the Gospel of John? Indisputably one part
of Polycarp's testimony relative to John's Gospel carries us back to John himself. For Polycarp's evidence respecting the work of his
teacher must be based upon the testimony of
his teacher himself. The case becomes all the
more clear the more closely we look into it on
the adversaries' side, and range ourselves with
those who deny the validity of John's Gospel.
According to this view, Polycarp, although saying so much to Irenæus regarding John, did
not drop a word regarding the Gospel of John.
But supposing he did not, is it credible that
Irenæus fully accepted that Gospel, that work
which seemed to be the noblest gift of John to
Christianity, the report of an eye-witness respecting the life, death, and resurrection of the
Saviour of the world, as a Gospel which ran directly counter to the testimony of the three
other evangelists? Would not the very circumstance that Polycarp made no mention of
it have convinced Irenæus of its want of authenticity? And yet it is asserted that in order
to meet and overthrow false teachers, and the

men who falsified the canon, he did not hesitate to reckon the Gospel of John as strictly embraced among the sacred books.

This on which I am now laying stress is nothing new ; it has long stood recorded on the pages of Irenæus, and has long been read there But it has not had its due weight ; else how could it have been so lightly passed over ? For my own part I must completely justify the assigning of much greater weight, on the part of correct and thorough investigators, to the testimony of Polycarp and Irenæus respecting the Gospel of John, than to all the difficulties and all the objections urged by skeptical scholars.

And is the case not similar with Tertullian and his testimony respecting the Gospel ? This man, who had been transformed from a worldly heathen lawyer into a powerful advocate of divine truth, enters so critically into the question of the origin and relative value of the four Gospels as expressly to subordinate Mark and Luke to Matthew and John, on the ground that the former were mere helpers and companions of the apostles, while the latter were se-

lected by the Lord himself and invested with
full authority.[23] The same author propounds
also an inexpugnable canon of historical criticism, a test of the truth of the early Christian
documents, and especially those of apostolic
origin, in that he makes the value of testimony
dependent on the epoch of the witness, and de-
mands that what was held as true in his day
should be judged in the light of its prior acceptance. If it had been accepted before, it was
fair to suppose that it had been equally accepted
in the time of the apostles; its authenticity
must therefore have been admitted by the apostolical church, founded as it was by the apostles
themselves.[24] And is it to be believed that this
acute man was capable of being deceived in his
acceptance of the Gospels and in his defense of
them by any thin web of sophistry or touch of
charlatanism? The passages just referred to
are taken from his celebrated reply to Marcion,
who in a wanton and heretical spirit had impugned the authenticity of the Gospels. Three
of the four he had wholly excluded, and of the
fourth he retained only just so much as it pleased

him to do. In replying to him, Tertullian expressly bases his argument on the ground that at
the time when the apostolical church was founded all the four Gospels were accredited. Has
such a statement no weight in the mouth of a
man like Tertullian ? When he wrote, scarcely
a hundred years had elapsed since the death of
John. At that date the testimony, appealed
to by him, of the church at Ephesus, in which
John had labored so long and amid which he
had died, must have been full and decisive respecting the genuineness or spuriousness of
John's Gospel. Nor was it a matter of any
difficulty to ascertain what was the judgment
which this church passed on the Gospel. And
we must not overlook the fact that we have not
to do, in this matter, with a scholar who is con-
tenting himself with merely learned investigations, but with a man full of earnestness respecting his faith, and taking very seriously the
question of human salvation. The Christian
documents which asserted a connection between
themselves and the origin of the new faith, the
documents at which all the worldly wisdom of

the time in which Tertullian himself was reared
took offense, — were they likely to be accepted
by him without inquiry, and in a blind credulity ? And inasmuch as he expressly assures
us that he bases his acceptation of all the four
Gospels on the credit of the apostolical church,[25]
is it not an unworthy suspicion, the doubting
that he made thorough inquiry into the capacity
of the apostolical church to pass an authentic
judgment on the Christian documents ?

I insist therefore, to sum up the matter, that
the testimony of Irenæus and· Tertullian respecting the four Gospels is not to be taken as
an isolated, unrelated fact, but that it must be
considered as a valid result of all the historical
evidence which was at their command. And
how far we are justified in this, is shown not
only by the authorities already adduced, the
author of the Muratori list of New Testament
books, the African translator of the Gospels
into Latin, the originator of the Itala, but by
all the other witnesses who lived prior to the
time of Irenæus and Tertullian.

Many of my readers are acquainted with the

so-called Harmonies of the Gospels, — the works
in which the four sacred narratives are co-ordinated into a single one.   In this way an effort
has been made to draw from the Gospels alone
a closely followed and faithful portrait of our
Lord's life, those points which one narrator has
brought more prominently into view than the
others being employed as supplementary to the
other accounts, and a complete picture being
the result.   In these works the narrative of
John has been drawn upon to supply the inci-
dents occurring in the last three years of Jesus'
life, and to follow his course step by step.
Harmonies of this kind were prepared as early
as the year 170 by two men whose names are
known to us: one of them was Theophilus,
Bishop of Antioch in Syria;   the other was
Tatian, a disciple of Justin the great theologian and martyr.[26]   True, both of those works
are lost; but Jerome speaks in the fourth century of the one prepared by Theophilus as still
existing, describing it as a combination of the
four Gospels in one continuous narrative;[27] respecting the second we have the testimony of

Eusebius [28] and Theodoret,[29] the latter of whom
speaks with intimate knowledge. Tatian himself alludes to his work as " the Gospel made
up of four, the Diatessaron." Both of these
men wrote other works which are still extant.
In 180 and 181 Theophilus indited the three
books to Autolycus, a learned heathen who had
assailed Christianity. In this work are extracts from Matthew, Luke, and John. It is
especially noteworthy that he cites the latter
(ii. 22), alluding explicitly to the name of the
author. His words are, " This is taught by the
Holy Scriptures and all inspired men, among
whom is John, who says, ' In the beginning was
the Word, and the Word was with God,' and
then follows, ' and the Word was God : all
things were made by him, and without him
was not anything made that was made.' "
This makes it certain that the Harmony of Theophilus embraced the Gospel of John.[30] The
same is true of Tatian : for in his Addresses to
the Heathen, a work filled with learning, and
very decided in its tone, written probably between 166 and 170, there are several passages

quoted from John's Gospel, such as this : " The
Light shineth in darkness, and the darkness
comprehendeth it not. . . . . The Life was the
Light of men. . . . . All things were made by
him, and without him was not anything made
that was made." From this it would seem certain that his Harmony, like that of Theophilus,
although it may have taken some liberties with
the order of the narrative, included the Gospel
of John : and this chimes admirably with the
statement of Bishop Bar Salibi, that the Diatessaron of Tatian, accompanied by a commentary
by Ephraim, and thus discriminated from the
Diatessaron of Ammonius, began with the
words, " In the beginning was the Word."

These Harmonies last mentioned, one of which
must with much probability be ascribed to a
date within the first sixty years of the second
century, have far more worth than what would
be gathered from single scattered extracts, for
their preparation points back conclusively to a
time when the four Gospels were already accepted as a perfect record, and when the necessity had begun to be felt of deducing a higher

unity and a more harmonious completeness
from them than the diversity of the various
books and the apparent discrepancies had rendered apparent. If these efforts are to be assigned to a date as early as the second decade
subsequently to the middle of the second century, it makes the inference a necessary one
that the use and recognition of the four Gospels
must be assigned to a much earlier date.

Similar testimony we owe to a cotemporary of
the two men just named, Claudius Apollinaris,
Bishop of Hierapolis in Phrygia, whose epoch
is assigned by Eusebius (iv. 26) to the reign of
Marcus Aurelius. For in a fragment preserved
in the Chronicon Paschale he declares that if
the Quartodecimanians (so called from holding
like the Jews that the fourteenth of Nisan was
the day for celebrating the paschal sacrifice)
appeal justly to Matthew in support of the view
that Jesus partook of the last supper with his
disciples at the precise time of celebrating the
paschal offering, there must be an antagonism
among the writers of the several Gospels. Now
as in this contest Matthew, Mark, and Luke

4

must be ranged on the one side, and John on
the other, the words of Apollinaris indicate
that all the Gospels were conceded in his day
to have equal value. To this may be added
that in one passage still extant in the same
Chronicon there is undeniable reference to
John's allusion (xix. 34) to the piercing of
Jesus' side.

According to Eusebius, the choice of Dionysius as Bishop of Corinth occurred in the year
170. The same historian has preserved for us
(Euseb. iv. 23) some fragments of letters and
other documents from the pen of Dionysius.
To one church he sent in the epistolary form
expositions of Scripture; and to the Romans
he wrote, after animadverting severely upon
the efforts to discredit the genuineness of his
own letters, that it was not at all strange that
men sought to discredit the Gospels, since these
too were documents whose value was so great
that their authenticity should be indisputable.
The expression, Holy Scriptures, might not necessarily refer to the New Testament; but the
word which Dionysius employs — writings re-

specting the Lord,— the same term which Clemens of Alexandria uses (Strom. vii. 1) — has the same signification with the expression New Testament, and relates evidently to the books which were then accepted as constituting the New Testament canon.

The Apology written by Athenagoras of Athens, in the year 177, contains several quotations from Matthew and Luke ; it displays also unmistakable marks of being influenced by John's Gospel; as, for example, in the passages which speak of the Logos as the Word of God, and which allude to the Son of God who is in the Father as the Father is in the Son. It contains the very expression found in the first chapter of John, third verse, " All things were made by him," and in the seventeenth chapter, twenty-first verse, " as thou, Father, art in me and I in thee."

I have taken these witnesses to the credibility of our Gospels from the epoch prior to Irenæus and Tertullian, and just at the threshold of the Irenæan period, the second and third decade after the middle of the second century

There are, however, left to us other witnesses
much earlier, and, like those just quoted, men
who speak to us right from the very bosom of
the church.[31]

Between the apostolic epoch and that which
followed there intervene the so-called apostolic
Fathers; for as direct disciples of the apostles
they must be reckoned as in immediate connection with the apostolic age. If in the little which
these men have left us we do not find anything
which can be construed as definite testimony as
to the authenticity of the Gospels, still we are
not to conclude from their silence that the Gospels were not in existence before their time. But
should there be in their writings a constant
use of the Old Testament, and not the slightest
use of the New, in spite of the fact that the
latter lay so much nearer to hand,[32] the probability must be accepted as great that at that
time the Gospels were not accepted as of equal
weight with the Old Testament.

And this appears to have been the case with
the epistle of the Roman Clement, written in
the second or third decade before the close of

the first century, and about a decade after the
destruction of Jerusalem. At that time no
canon of the Gospels was in existence. It is
indeed unquestionable that in his epistle, rich
in quotations from the Old Testament, Clement
refers here and there to passages[33] in the Pauline Epistles, which have indeed chronologically
priority over the Gospels, though not in any
other sense.[34]

It is otherwise with those other constituents
of this literature to whose discussion we now
come, — the epistles of Ignatius and that of
Polycarp. The first of these have reached us
various in extent and variously edited. Three
extant only in Latin are manifestly later additions to the older literature ; and so too are five
others, written in Greek, Latin, and Armenian,
their authenticity being disowned by the fact
that Eusebius makes no allusion to them.
There are besides seven epistles, which are extant in a longer and a shorter form : of the
longer one, there is also an ancient Latin version ; of the shorter, a Latin version and Syriac,
and Armenian ones as well. With this is to

be joined the fact that twenty years ago a Syriac version of three of these seven epistles was
discovered, more brief than the short Greek
text. After the debate respecting the longer
and the shorter epistles had been decisively settled in favor of the shorter, the question arose
whether the three extant in the Syriac translation are not to be preferred to these seven
shorter ones. When several scholars declared
themselves in favor of this, others defended the
earlier origin of the seven Greek epistles, insisting that the three in Syriac were a mere
extract, intended for devotional uses. We hold
this to be the more correct view. Similar
occurrences are not unknown in the apocryphal
writings of the New Testament. An extraordinary proof in this case is afforded by the circumstance that these seven epistles are not
only recognized by Eusebius (iii. 36), but are
alluded to in the letter of Polycarp. In order
to escape the force of this testimony, the most
decisive passage in the latter epistle, defended
as it is by Eusebius himself, must be set aside
as unauthentic. Besides this, the assigning of

superior value to the three Syriac letters is invalidated by the fragmentary character of many passages; one is so manifestly an excerpt from the Greek text that it must be admitted that one section has been lost through the carelessness of the copyist. We claim the right, therefore, of holding to the authenticity of the seven epistles ascribed by Eusebius and Polycarp to Ignatius, and written while he was on the way from Antioch, through Smyrna and Troas, to his martyrdom at Rome. Examining them with reference to our present theme, we find several allusions to Matthew and John. Take this passage (letter to the Romans, chap. 6): "For what is a man profited if he shall gain the whole world and lose his own soul?" taken literally from Matt. xvi. In like manner, the passage in his epistle to the people of Smyrna, in which he asserts of Jesus that he was baptized by John "in order that all righteousness might be fulfilled by him," reminds one of Matt. iii. 15: "for thus it becometh us to fulfill all righteousness." In the letter to the Romans (chap. 7), he writes, "I want the bread of God, the bread of heaven, the bread of life, which is the body of Jesus Christ the Son of God ; . . . and I want the draught of God, the blood of Jesus, which is imperishable love and eternal life." Compare this with the sixth chapter of John, verse 41 : " I am the bread which came down from heaven ; " verse 48 : " I am that bread of life ; " verse 51 : " And the bread that I will give is my flesh ; " verse 54 : " Whoso eateth my flesh and drinketh my blood hath eternal life." To the Philadelphians he writes (chap. 7), " What if some wished to lead me astray after the flesh ? but the Spirit is not enticed ; he is from God ; he knows wherever he cometh and whither he goeth, and he brings to punishment that which is hidden." These verses have as their basis John iii. 6 to 8,[35] while the last clause grows out of the twentieth [36] verse. Were these allusions of Ignatius to Matthew and John a mere isolated phenomenon, and one which would be adverse to other points in this discussion on which no doubts rest, they would not have decisive weight. But so far from militating against other points of evidence, they are in full agreement with them, particularly in view of the fact that at the time when the letters were written, between 107, the date generally assigned, and 115, they contain references to two of the most important of the four Gospels.

The letter of Polycarp to the Philippians connects itself most closely with those of Ignatius. According to his own testimony, it was written very soon after the martyrdom of Ignatius; that is, between 107 and 115. It contains very brief quotations from Matthew, as, for example, in chap. 2: "Think on the Lord how he said, Judge not, that ye be not judged [Matt. vii. 1]. Forgive, and it shall be forgiven you [similar to Matt. vi. 14]. Be merciful, that you may obtain mercy [compare with Matt. v. 7]. And with what measure ye mete it shall be measured to you again [a literal quotation from Matt. vii. 2]. And blessed are the poor, and they which are persecuted for righteousness' sake; for theirs is the kingdom of heaven" [taken almost verbatim from Matt. v. 3 and 10]. Further, chap. 7: "We will implore

the Omniscient God not to lead us into temptation, remembering the words of the Lord,
The spirit is willing but the flesh is weak"
[compare Matt. vi. 13 and xxvi. 41]. Special
weight must be ascribed to that passage in
Polycarp's letter which clearly manifests the use
of the First Epistle of John. Polycarp writes,
chap. 7 : " For every one who does not confess
that Jesus Christ is come in the flesh is antichrist:" in John (iv. 3) the passage runs, "Every spirit that confesseth not that Jesus Christ is
come in the flesh is not of God ; and this is that
spirit of antichrist." The importance of this
use by Polycarp of the Epistle of John is based
upon this, that — although the heroes of doubt
bring into suspicion even that which is really
indisputable — the Epistle and the Gospel of
John are shown, by their essential unity of incident and language, to have necessarily had
the same author ; and thus the use of the Epistle argues the use of the Gospel as well. I
have shown above, from Polycarp's intimate
relation to John, how valuable is his testimony:
it has such great weight as scarcely to allow a

word to be uttered in disavowal of the writings
which he confirms. The unworthy skill of
modern scholars has not shrunk, however, from
setting aside the fact of Polycarp's testimony
and unnerving its strength. A writer of much
acuteness says, " We are not compelled to regard the words of Polycarp as an actual quotation from John, for that may have been a sentence which had come into circulation in the
church, and may have been committed to paper
by John just as well as by Polycarp, without
compelling the latter to learn it from the former." Before this conjecture had been bruited, a fellow-believer had fallen upon another
way out of the difficulty : " Can the thing not
be reversed ? May not the author of the Johannean Gospel, which is as little genuine as so
much else that has for two thousand years received the reverent homage of Christendom, —
may not this false John have cited as well from
Polycarp ? " It requires a great deal of courage
to give utterance to such an idle fancy ; yet
there are men of learning who are not lacking
in this courage. But the universal and radical

medicament which must be relied on at the
last admits in this instance of a double application. If the Gospel of John can be thrown
overboard so easily, the Epistle of Polycarp can
not so readily be disposed of. Polycarp, then,
did not write the epistle. Yet the disciple of
Polycarp, Irenæus, believed and gave his witness to just the contrary. But there are never
lacking specious grounds for a false position;
and the professors of the nineteenth century
have the art of putting out of sight even an
Irenæus and his fellows.

The attack on the authenticity of Polycarp's
epistle is all the more worth refuting, because,
if successful, it does away no less with the genuineness of Ignatius's epistles, all the more
troublesome if they are to be accepted in the
limits which Polycarp and Eusebius assigned to
them. On this account the latest outbreaks of
critical presumption and audacity have been
directed against the whole Polycarp-Ignatius
literature. What one of these critical heroes
does not venture, another does. One goes to
work more in " root and branch " fashion, an-

other more artistically. The one contents himself with rejecting on his own authority all
those passages in Polycarp's letter which allude
to the person and epistles of Ignatius, imputing
them to a forger known to have lived long before Eusebius's time; the other, on the contrary,
casts away the whole letter. In like manner,
the one satisfies himself with regarding the
three shortest Syrian epistles of Ignatius as
genuine; the other holds it more advisable to
assert that not a single one of the collective letters of Ignatius is genuine. Such dealings as
this would soon convert the temple of God into
a common ruin.

For my own part, I do not hesitate to advance
further in the period of Polycarp. Justin the
Martyr, even before his violent death in Rome
in 166 made his memory dear to the church,
had attained to great celebrity through his
writings. Three of his works are still extant
in the complete form, and their authenticity is
undisputed, — the two apologies and the dialogue with the Jew Tryphon. Eusebius displays perfect familiarity with the two which

were written to defend Christianity against the
attacks of high pagan authorities, and speaks
of them as two separate works, one of which
was dedicated to the Emperor Antoninus, the
other to Marcus Aurelius. Jerome repeats the
statement of Eusebius, and most scholars [37]
down to the present day have coincided with
him. The first work must be assigned to the
year 138 or 139, the other to the year 161, the
first year of the reign of Marcus Aurelius.
Respecting the first, however, it should be said
that it was in 139 that Marcus Aurelius (Beris-
simus) was named as Cæsar, yet the inscription
does not address him with the imperial title.
Very recently there have been new views taken
respecting· this matter, and there has been
unjustified evidence [38] brought forward to support the assigning of the year 147 [39] to the production of the first of the two works in question : some, moreover, have felt themselves justified in taking a position not warranted by
Eusebius and Jerome, and in regarding the
second apology as no independent production,
but a mere appendix to the first. Neither the

one view nor the other appears to me to be
thoroughly grounded. Still, the value of Justin's testimony is very little affected by the question whether he wrote a few years prior or subsequently to the year 140. Yet the fact that
these two works of Justin's were written prior
to the middle of the second century makes the
question one of great interest whether he discussed our Gospels in them. It is a topic which
has been treated in our time by many persons,
and with great variance of opinion. What is
the essential result gained from these investigations ? That Justin often quotes from our own
Matthew, is indisputable.[40] That in various
passages he follows Mark and Luke, is extremely
probable.[41] Yet this fact has been invalidated
by the efforts of some to show that Justin did
not use our Gospels as his basis, but writings
very like them in character, perhaps the Gospel of the Hebrews, or, according to some, the
Gospel of Peter, which was derived from the
latter, but which, with the exception of a few
passages,[42] has remained entirely unknown to
us to the present time. One support for this

view is found in the fact that some quotations
of Justin are also found in the pseudo-Clementine homilies, having there the same or similar
differences from the readings in the canonical
text.[43] The supposition is, perhaps, an admis-
sible one, that Justin, at the very earliest times,
drew that Gospel of the Hebrews, which contained such repeated references to Matthew,
into the circle of his evangelical quotations in
one of his first works; for we have Eusebius's
authority, in the first half of the fourth century,
for the fact that at his time this Gospel was
reckoned by several authorities as belonging to
the canon.   On the other hand, it is a manifest and groundless exercise of arbitrary authority to hold that such of his quotations as
harmonize more or less closely with our received
text are taken from a source respecting which
we are left to conjecture alone.   Such a view is
all the more inadmissible from the fact that
free extracts from our Gospels are fully in accordance with the character of the times in
which they fall; and this is the same epoch,
the first half of the second century, to which

we trace the main origin of the diverse materials which enter into the canon, and more especially the Gospels. With equal freedom Justin makes his quotations from the Old Testament, even if he may not be proved to take his
text exclusively from the standard Septuagint.
And the fact is not to be overlooked, that the
passages quoted by Justin from the Gospels can
not be judged by the documents comprising the
New Testament text which has come down to
us, and which forms the substance of our usual
editions ; it is clear that many of our most
widely diffused readings have proceeded from
earlier or more recent corruptions in the primitive text; the Gospels especially were subject
to arbitrary changes within the very first ten
years after they had been committed to writing.[44]

My discussion thus far of the extracts which
Justin makes from the Gospels relates solely to
those which he draws from the synoptic ones,
the first three. Despite the prevailing skepticism in this matter, it is as good as certain that
Justin made use of those three Gospels : but

5

all the more obstinate is the assertion that he had no acquaintance with John's Gospel. But what in fact is his relation to John ? In my opinion there are most cogent reasons for believing that John was read and used by Justin. The delineation of the person of Christ, characteristic of John, as, for example, in the opening of the Gospel, "In the beginning was the Word, and the Word was with God, and the Word was God," and in verse fourteen, " And the Word became flesh," as well as the general designation of Jesus as the Logos or Word of God,[45] appears unmistakably in not a few passages in Justin, such, for instance, as " And Jesus Christ was begotten in a manner wholly peculiar to himself as the Son of God, while he is also the Word (Logos) of the same." " The primeval force (δύναμις) after the Father of All and God the Lord, is the Son, the Word (Logos) ; and I shall show how he through the incarnation (σαρκοποιηθεὶς) became man." " The Word (Logos) of God is the Son of the same." " As they have not confessed all that belongs to the Logos, which is Christ, they have

often uttered what is at variance with itself."
" Through the Word (Logos) of God, Jesus
Christ our Saviour became flesh (σαρκοποιηθεὶς)."
To these passages, taken from the brief second
Apology, I add the following, taken from the
first (chap. 33) : " By the expressions the
Holy Ghost and the Power of God in Luke i. 35
[the Holy Ghost shall come upon thee and the
power of the Highest shall overshadow thee],
we are to understand the Logos, which is the
first begotten of God." In the " Dialogue,"
chap. 105, we find that " the same was begotten
by the Father of All after a peculiar manner
as the Word (Logos) and Power (δύναμις), becoming flesh through the instrumentality of
the Virgin Mary, as we learn from the memori-
als which I have already displayed." In order
to invalidate the proof found here that Justin
wrote not independently of John, critics have
made an effort to point out the differences between the conceptions of Logos which they both
maintained, and to show that Justin had a su-
perficial and merely external view of it. But
is it to be supposed that those who first accepted

the doctrines of John were able to fathom and
exhaust them all ? On the contrary, does not
the fact that Justin was not able to penetrate
to the depths of John's theology show that in
his very allusions to it, without fully comprehending it, he was not independent of it ? It
seems to me that the internal connection between both meets the opponents of the authenticity of John's Gospel in no more convincing
manner than in showing how the doctrines
of John may be culled from the words of
Justin.[46]

There are not wanting passages in John's
Gospel, moreover, which may be found specifically reproduced in Justin. In the " Dialogue,"
chap. 88, he writes of John the Baptist, " The
people believed that he was the Christ ; but he
said to them, I am not Christ, but the voice
of a preacher." This is in direct connection
with the words of John i. 20 and 23 ; for the
first words in the reply of the Baptist have been
reported by no other evangelist than John.

Twice can Justin's expressions only be explained by supposing him to have been familiar

with the account in John ix. of the man who
had been born blind. He speaks expressly of
the miraculous healings effected by Jesus, and
says in the first Apology (chap. 22) that the
Saviour restored to health one who was born
lame, palsied, and blind.[47] In like manner in
the "Dialogue" (chap. 69) he declares that
Jesus healed those who were blind, deaf, and
lame from their birth,[48] giving to one sound
limbs, to another hearing, to a third restored
sight. What a trick of art is it to take the
words "I was born blind,"[49] spoken by the man
who was a defender of Christ, and who corresponds to the blind man of Jericho, and to
make them refer to an unknown source used
by Justin, an ostensibly lost authority of the
narrative which he gives elsewhere! To what
end is this? To no other than to discredit the
Gospel of John, and to deny that it was before
Justin when he wrote.

The words of Zechariah xii. 10 Justin quotes
(first Apology, 52; also "Dialogue," 14 and
33) precisely in the language of John xix. 37,
"they shall look on him whom they pierced."

The text of the Seventy, which Jerome expressly confirms, has an entirely different translation[50] of this passage ; yet there is one of the
older versions given us by Aquila, Symmachus,
and Theodotion, which coincides with the language of John and Justin. There is nothing
more improbable than that John and Justin
were here independent of each other, and followed a translation of the Hebrew text which
is unknown to us. Is the acceptance of this
theory, one of the most untenable of positions,
taken to avoid the manifest connection between
the words of Justin and those of John ?

To close this part of our discussion, we find
in Justin's first Apology, chap. 61, Christ has
said, " Unless ye are born again, ye can not enter the kingdom of heaven. It is manifest to
every one that those who have been born once
can not enter again into their mother's womb."
This passage has been the theme of much con-
troversy ; but I am fully of the opinion that
Justin had in view the passage in John iii. 3 to
5, " Verily, verily, I say unto thee, Except a
man be born again,[51] he can not see the king-

dom of God.[52]   Nicodemus saith unto him,
How can a man be born when he is old ?   Can
he enter the second time into his mother's
womb and be born ?   Jesus answered, Verily,
verily, I say unto thee, Except a man be born
of water and of the Spirit he can not enter
into the kingdom of God " [kingdom of heaven
according to the Sinaitic Codex and other ancient authorities.]   Now what means is there
of escaping the inference which the parallelism
in these two passages gives rise to ?   Those
who have attempted to do this have quoted Matt.
xviii. 3, " Verily I say unto you, Except ye be
converted, and become as little children, ye
shall not enter into the kingdom of heaven,"
and have given utterance to the suspicion that
in some lost Gospel, perhaps that of the
Hebrews, to which reference has already been
made, this passage was recorded just as Justin
has given it, his authority therefor being not
John, but some previous writer.[53]   In order
therefore to avoid what lies directly in our
path, we are compelled to have recourse to
some unknown higher authority.   The second

part of Justin's expression gives all the less
reason for appealing from John to Matthew, that
the fifth verse in the passage in John (standing in direct connection with the third), "he
can not enter into the kingdom of heaven"
[Himmelreich], is the apparent basis of
Justin's expression, "ye can not enter into
the kingdom of heaven." The phrase "kingdom of God" was completely overshadowed by
the more usual one, kingdom of heaven.[54] Decisive too of the personal use of John by
Justin is that expression of the latter relative
to the entering again into the mother's womb
and being born, derived from John iii. 4. To
suppose such a coincidence of thought and language to have been accidental, is a feat of
trickery which can deceive no one capable of
forming an independent judgment.

To this result, which confirms the authenticity of the first three Gospels as much as it does
the fourth, I must add two points more, which
still strengthen my conclusions. One of these
is, that Justin is in the habit of alluding to
the " Memorabilia of the Apostles, known as

Gospels," without specifically mentioning the
names of the authors. Yet while doing this he
makes particular mention of the fact that the
writers were apostles[55] and companions of Jesus, and by speaking of their combined writings as the " Gospel " he leads us to the un-
doubting conviction that it was invested with
full canonical authority: and such an investi-
ture naturally allows the names of the writers to fall into the background and to be
unnoticed, while their writings might have
general acceptance. In the second place, we
have to notice that Justin, even in his first
Apology (chap. 67), asserts that in the Christian congregations the " Memorabilia of the
Apostles or the writings of the Prophets " were
read every Sunday. Here then is an instance
of the Gospels and the prophetical books being
placed on the same plane, the first being exalted to the same canonicity which the latter
had enjoyed from the first. It is an error or a
self-deception to deny that Justin's words do
not warrant the acceptance of those books as
canonical, on the ground that there were writ-

ings read in the church which were not accepted as a part of the canon. There were
such books indeed, but they formed a class
subordinate to the canon, and pre-supposing
the formation of it. Of course there was not
at the outset an immediate recognition of the
equality of the Christian records with the hallowed books of the Old Testament; but after
the church had enlarged the canon by admitting those sacred writings which had sprung
from a common source, and had given them
equal honor with those previously accepted,
there came into view certain books which had
more or less claim to recognition as canonical:
and thus it came about that some were admitted to the prerogative of being read in the
churches, without sharing the same honor
which was given to those accepted as fully canonical. At a later period the church found it
to be for its interest to assign to these books, to
which usage gave a kind of half-canonical character, a rank equal to the highest. That this
does not apply in the least to the earliest formation of the Christian canon is shown by the

Muratori Fragment which speaks of the Apocalypse of John and of Peter. We accept these, but the last named is not admitted by some of our scholars to the honor of being publicly read in church. This doubt expresses distinctly the want of full canonical authority which led to the rejection of the writing in question. Later usage can not do away with this ; and just as little can the fact that in some instances the direct relation of a paper to a single congregation became a source of advantage to the common church, as is testified by Dionysius of Corinth (Euseb., Hist. Eccl. iv. 23) in the case of the letters of Clemens and Soter to the Corinthians. In the Muratori Fragment already referred to, it is stated, toward the end of the Shepherd of Hermas, that he was to be recommended for private use, but not for public worship, and that he was to be included neither in the number of prophets nor apostles.

The manner in which Justin expresses himself in the passage quoted above (first Apology, chap. 67) makes it impossible, in my opinion, to doubt that in his time the Gospels were ac-

cepted as of canonical authority. We possess
in fact a much earlier testimony of this equality in one of the generally accepted seven
short letters, in that to Smyrna, the seventh
chapter, where are the words, " It behooves us
to give heed to the prophets, and especially to
the Gospel, in which the passion and the resurrection are fully portrayed." Here too, as
the reader observes, there is a manifest coup-
ling of the prophets and the authors of the Gospels, i. e. the books which in their full extent and
defined limits form the Gospel, and a proof
that both were in common use in the church.[56]

These are proofs from the first quarter (whether the year be taken as 107 or 115) and from the
second quarter (139, or, as some suppose, ten
years earlier) of the second century, that at
that time the Gospels were held as of equal
validity with the prophets, and were admitted
to canonical authority, a place being assigned
them directly after the prophetical books.
What is not told us in detail respecting the
various Gospels may be inferred from many
other testimonies. I have already shown, from

various passages of Justin Martyr's undisputed
writings, that our Gospels, without the exception of the fourth, that of John, were admitted
to form one GOSPEL, and to be invested with
canonical authority. Is it possible, therefore, for
the opinion to be justified that at Justin's time
other Gospels than ours were in use as having
had a sacred origin, in spite of the fact that,
decades after Justin, these, and no others,
were in repute through the whole Christian
church? Does it not contravene all that we
know of the origin of the canon, that at the
outset, and even in the age of Justin, only
Matthew, Mark, and Luke were regarded as
canonical, and that John was subsequently
smuggled in?

According to the views of many, Justin was
the author of the Letter to Diognetus; but those
who assign to this an earlier date, and consider it the work of an older cotemporary of
Justin's, are more correct. Although this short
apologetic epistle contains no definite quotation
from any one of the Gospels, it contains many
allusions to evangelical passages, and especially

to John. The words of the sixth chapter,
" Christians live in the world, but are not of
the world ; " those of the tenth, " for God has
loved men, for whom he created the world ;
. . . . to whom he has sent his only-begotten Son," contain almost unmistakable references to John xvii. 11, " these are in the
world ; " '14, " the world hateth them, for they
are not of the world ; " 16, " they are not of the
world, even as I am not of the world ; " and to
John iii. 16, " for God so loved the world that
he gave his only-begotten Son."

But before advancing further we must come
back to the Gospel of the Hebrews, whose use
in connection with our synoptic Gospels is rendered probable by the language of Justin, by
the pseudo-Clementine, and even by Tatian's
Diatessaron, or Harmony of the Gospels, and
testified by Eusebius (iv. 22: 3) of Hegesippus.
Does not this bring into great uncertainty the
character of the earlier Gospel canon ? It certainly appears to do so if the Gospel of the
Hebrews is admitted to a place side by side
with the synoptic Gospels, and be regarded

as an independent production. Against such a
view there are a variety of considerations to be
urged. I have already mentioned that the
authorship of this Gospel was ascribed to Matthew. We shall see, further on, that at a very
early period, in its original Hebrew form, it was
held to be the work of Matthew, and that Greek
editions, with many changes in the text, were
in use among the judaizing Christians. This
has led to the result that the passages of the
Gospel of the Hebrews which have been transmitted to us from antiquity, and more especially
those which have recently been brought to light[57]
by the writer of these pages, manifest a striking
parallelism with our Gospel of Matthew. All
these circumstances lead to the conviction that
at the beginning, and probably during the first
half of the second century, the Gospel of Matthew and that of the Hebrews were regarded
not as essentially different productions, but as
different editions of the same document, and
that by degrees greater light was diffused regarding the variations in them. Thus Irenæus
states of the Ebionites, in two passages (i. 26:

2 ; iii. 11 : 7), that they made use of the Gospel
of Matthew ; while Eusebius (iii. 27), probably
referring to the first of these passages, corrects
Irenæus's statement, and puts the Gospel of the
Hebrews in the place of that of Matthew. Yet
it happened, near the end of the fourth century,
that the most learned theologian and most experienced critic of his age, Jerome, while in
possession of the Gospel of the Hebrews in the
Syro-Chaldaic dialect of the country, and full
of the recollections of an older tradition, believed that it was the original text of Matthew
fallen into his hands. After becoming more
fully acquainted with it, and after translating it
into Latin and Greek, he acknowledged that
many believed that it was the work of Matthew
himself.

Thus far we have been concerned almost exclusively with the writings of men in whom the
church, from the second century, in which they
lived, onward, recognized venerated pillars of
the faith. Yet at the same epoch there was a
rich literature, which, in conjunction with what
was ecclesiastical, put forth a rank growth,

which elevated far above the simple Christian
doctrine a system of speculations evolved from
the schools of heathen and Jewish philosophy:
I refer to the heretical views which became
current, and which may be also known as the
doctrines of the Errorists. Even from this literature we derive convincing proofs that by the
middle, or even before the middle of the second
century, our Gospels had attained the highest
degree of consideration. This is interesting
not more for the light which it throws upon the
earlier history of heresy than for that which it
sheds upon the age and the origin of our Gospels. In calling upon these errorists to give
evidence respecting the Gospels, we have no
less an authority than Irenæus, that Bishop of
Lyons of whom I have elsewhere spoken in detail. Irenæus himself utters the expression,
" So firmly are our Gospels grounded, that even
the errorists are compelled to acknowledge
their credibility, and each one of them must
begin with them in order to lay the foundations
of his own system." [53] This is a judgment
passed by the second half of the second century

on the character of the first half. And this
first half of the second century is just the period
to which the opponents of the genuineness of
our Gospels are accustomed to appeal. Now, are
we to suppose that a man like Irenæus, who lived
only a few decades after the period to which I
am referring, was not better acquainted with the
facts than the scholars and professors of the
nineteenth century? The more the respect due
to the true progress of science in our age, the
less is owed to those scholars who employ their
knowledge and acumen for the purpose of
thrusting at truth. The accuracy of what Irenæus testified to can be substantiated even to-
day with facts; and our tread is all the more
secure if we do not withhold our belief. What
the earliest Fathers have testified respecting the
primitive errorists (and to the hints of the former we owe the larger share of our knowledge
about the latter), shows us, in the most convincing manner, how radically separate they
were from the Gospels; and from the books
which were considered holy- by the church.
Irenæus himself is one of the chief preservers

of these indications; after him comes a work (discovered only twenty years ago) of a disciple of Irenæus, Hippolytus by name, a man who lived so nearly cotemporaneously with those errorists as to warrant being received as equally good authority as Irenæus regarding them.

One of the boldest and most gifted thinkers among those errorists was Valentinus,[59] who came from Egypt to Rome about the year 140, and resided there for the twenty years succeeding. He undertook the task of writing a complete history of those " supernal transactions which took place in the realm of the divine primeval Powers and supernatural Being before the sending of the only-begotten of the Father," hoping to be able to determine the better from the character of these events the nature and mission of the Son of God. In carrying out this stupendous design, he did not overlook the humble task of culling from John's Gospel a great number of conceptions and expressions, such as the Only-Begotten, the Word, Light, Life, Fullness, Truth, Grace, Saviour, Comfort-

er, and of using them for his purpose. There
is in this such an undeniable connection between the Gospel of John and the edifice of
Valentine's construction that only two explanations of it are possible. Either Valentine made
use of John or John of Valentine. The latter
alternative, according to my previously stated
views of the second century, must be regarded
as pure nonsense, and closer investigation into
the matter confirms this. If science, hostile to
the church, is able to reconcile itself to this
fact, it passes judgment on itself. Irenæus
states explicitly that the sect of Valentine made
the fullest use of the Gospel of John;[60] and he
gives the most explicit demonstration that the
first chapter of John was drawn upon for one
of the main features of the Valentinian system,
the doctrine of the first Ogdoade.[61] The statement of Irenæus confirms that of Hippolytus,
for he cites expressions of John which Valentine
had quoted. This is the most clearly the case
with John x. 8; for Hippolytus writes, " Whereas the prophets and the law, according to Valentine's belief, were filled with a subordinate

and foolish Spirit, Valentine says, ' The words
of the Saviour are, " All who came before me
are thieves and murderers." ' " [62]   And as the
Johannean, so were the other Gospels used by
Valentine. According to the statement of
Irenæus, he considered (i. 7 : 4) the subordinate
Spirit already mentioned, which he termed
Demiurgos and Taskmaster, to be represented
by the centurion of Capernaum (Matt. viii. 9 ;
Luke vii. 8) ; in the dead and resuscitated
twelve-year-old daughter of Jairus he recognized an image of his " sub-wisdom " (Acha-
moth), the mother of the Taskmaster (i. 8 : 2) ;
in like manner in the history of the woman
who had suffered for twelve years from an issue
of blood, and was healed by the Lord (Matt. ix.
20), he recognized the pains and restoration of
his twelfth primeval spirit (Æon) i. 3 : 3 ; and
the expression of Jesus recorded in Matt. v. 18
he applied to the ten æons hinted at in the
numerical value of the Iota, the smallest letter.

What do they who deny the high antiquity
of John's Gospel say to this ? They assert that
all that pertains to John was not brought out

by Valentine himself, but by his disciples. In fact, the expression is much more frequent in Irenæus "they say"—the followers of Valentine—than "he says," meaning Valentine himself. But who is wise enough to discriminate between what the master said and what the disciples added, without echoing their master in the least?[63] We must here touch once more upon the passage of Irenæus (iii. 11: 7) where he expresses himself respecting the relation of the heretics to the Gospels. After the sentence, "So securely are our Gospels founded, that even the errorists give testimony for them, and every one of these begins at the Gospels when he wants to try the foundations of his own system," he goes on to say, "For the errorists make exclusive use of the Gospel of Matthew, and are convinced from his pages alone of their error respecting the Lord. Marcion, however, avails himself of the mutilated Gospel according to Luke, and the very part which he retains makes his blasphemy against the only God apparent. Those who separate Jesus from Christ, and insist that it was Christ

alone, and not Jesus, who suffered, assign a
preference to the Gospel according to Mark.
If they read it with real love of truth, they can
be cured of their error ; but they who cleave to
Valentine make the fullest use of John's Gospel for the confirmation of their doctrine of
Æons ; and from this it can be seen that they
teach nothing correctly, as we have shown in
our first book." Does this representation of
Irenæus accord with the view that the use of
the Gospel according to John began with the
disciples of Valentine, and not with Valentine
himself? Irenæus declares the use of the
Johannean Gospel to have been a characteristic
feature of Valentine's school ; and those names
and conceptions already alluded to, which per-
vaded the whole system, testify convincingly to
this : yet was all this a mere affix to the system? So much respecting Irenæus. In Hippolytus the expression is even more definite
regarding Valentine. If now it is indisputable
that the author does not always discriminate
closely between the sect and the founder of the
sect, have we an example' of this in the case

now under consideration ? In those instances
where, in the course of a consecutive delineation, we are called upon to consider now the
founder and then the sect, is it not more logi-
cal to conclude that the founder and the sect
are to be taken as inseparably connected ?

From one disciple of Valentine's, Ptolemaus
by name, we receive a learned epistle, directed
to " Flora." In it, in conjunction with several
quotations from Matthew, is one from the first
chapter of John : " All things were made by
him (the Word), and without him was not
anything made that was made, says the apostle." The method employed to rob such quotations of their force is to make the errorists
who use these words as modern as possible; if
it be possible to trace them back only to the
close of the second century, the proofs drawn
from them do not acomplish anything more
than to substantiate what is already known,
that at that time, as the opponents of the church
gladly concede, the church in its ignorance had
fallen into the use of the canon of four Gospels.   But how recent was Ptolemaus's time ?

In all the most ancient sources he appears as
one of the most distingished and most influen-
tial disciples of Valentine's. As the epoch of
the latter was about the year 140, do we go too
far in setting the time of Ptolemaus at about
160 at the latest? Irenæus (in the second
book) and Hippolytus name him in connection
with Herakleon; and, in like manner, Pseudo-
Tertullian (in the affix to De præscriptionibus
hærticorum) and Philastrius place him directly
after Valentine. Irenæus in all probability
wrote the first and second books of his great
work before the year 180, and in both he concerns himself very much with Ptolemaus.

Here, however, we must bring in the testimony of Herakleon, the other very eminent
disciple of Valentine. Herakleon wrote an entire commentary on the Gospel of John; his
work is known to us through the many fragments which Origen has woven into his own
commentary on the same Gospel. From these
fragments it is plain that Herakleon's object
was carried out with consummate skill, to base
the assertions of his school on John: in this he

took the course which we have already remarked in Valentine. Wholly absorbed in his
own ideas, he found them reflected in a certain
double sense of Scripture which he traced particularly in John. In the passage, for example,
iii. 12, " after that, he withdrew to Capernaum," he held that there is an allusion to the
domain of material and worldly things to which
the Saviour condescended. The want of susceptibility in this domain of sense he thought
to be indicated by the fact that John has given
us no account of what Jesus said or did while
in Capernaum. The Samaritan woman at the
well of Jacob was to him the representative of
all souls which feel themselves drawn to what
is divine ; the water of Jacob's well, which
could not satisfy all spiritual necessities, was
the transitory Judaic economy. The man
whom the woman is required to summon is
her spiritual complement, her pleroma, her angel tarrying in the higher world of spirits. The
water which was offered to her indicates the divine life which was poured forth by the Saviour ;
the jar of the woman portrays her susceptibility

for this divine life. Is not this commentary
the most striking proof of the high authority
which the Gospel of John must have had even
then in the church, when the very errorists who
had turned away from the church so willingly
sought the confirmation of their own ideas in
it? And does not this show at a glance the
absurdity of the theory which derives John's
Gospel from the school of Valentine? But the
question recurs, How old is Herakleon? It is
one which has been urged with consummate
skill against our ancient sacred literature; and
the answer has been given with incredible
thoughtlessness, that he was the cotemporary
of Origen and of Hippolytus. Unquestionably
the oppressive weight of the matter under discussion has been experienced, and hence has
arisen the blindness to the evidences of antiquity
which are still in existence.[64]

Irenæus mentions Herakleon in connection
with Ptolemaus[65] in a way which shows him to
have been a well-known representative of the
school of Valentine. This acceptation of his
words is all the more fully justified by the fact

that he makes no further allusion to Herakleon. Clemens reminds us in the fourth book of his Stromata, written soon after the death of Commodus (193), of an interpretation given by Herakleon to Luke xii. 8, and terms him at the same time the most distinguished member [66] of Valentine's school. Origen states, at the commencement of his citations from Herakleon, that he was held to be a friend of Valentine's. [67] Hippolytus alludes to him in vi. 29 in the following words: "Valentinus and Herakleon and Ptolemaus and the whole school of these disciples of Pythagoras and Plato." Epiphanius says (Haer. 41), "Cerdo (the same who, according to Irenæus, iii. 4: 3, was with Valentine in Rome) follows these (the Ophites, Kainites, Sethians) and Herakleon." According to this evidence, Herakleon can not be assigned to a date more modern than 150 or 160. The expression which Origen has used of his relations to Valentine must, according to the usages of speech, be understood as applicable to a personal relation. [68] Epiphanius has certainly erred (an occurrence not often met in him) in letting Cerdo, whose epoch must be set at about 140, follow Herakleon ; but we have not the slightest right to suppose that he has made a mistake equal to the entire length of a man's life, and even more.[69]   And on this account we may rejoice in the fact that a Gnostic partisan wrote a complete commentary on the Gospel of John soon after the middle of the second century.

Had this Gospel then freshly appeared, and was it so flattering to the representatives of the Valentinian Gnosis that these gave it a cordial welcome ?   Assuredly it was no light task for them to draw out of the simple words of John their own profound system.   And it is not a little remarkable that the church thoroughly shared in the fancies of the errorists who had wandered so far out of the way.   In addition to this, there were those who knew that John had duly died at Ephesus without leaving behind any such legacy as a Gospel, and that such a work as it was could not have lain hid till that late day in a corner.   If the reader was not able to come to an understanding with him-

self in this wondrous thought-structure, he
only confirmed this fact, that the commentary
of Heralkeon is one of the strongest proofs that
then, when it was written, the Gospel of John
had long been revered as one of the hallowed
writings of the church, so that it seemed to
Herakleon a thing of special importance to show
that this apostolic document, if it should be
rightly interpreted, must be used to confirm the
system of Valentine.

While dealing with Valentine, or, according
to the order of time, before reaching Valentine,
we encounter Basilides, the period of whose
activity occurs, according to Eusebius, at the
epoch of Hadrian. With all his exhaustive
speculations on the Primeval, and the secret,
incomprehensible and lofty forces which spring
from it with living impulse, with all his med-
itations on the principles of light and darkness, life and death, his method of grasping
the subject of faith allied him by a close bond
with the adherents of the church, who stood on
a lower platform, so far as profession is concerned, than was the case with Valentine

One of his chief productions appears to be a commentary in twenty-four books on the Gospel. Eusebius (iv. 7) infers the existence of this work from the statements of a cotemporaneous opponent of Basilides, Agrippa Castor by name. Fragments from his book appear to have been preserved by Clemens, Origen, Epiphanius, and the so-called Archelaus Disputation. Has this work any relation to the subject now under review? It certainly appears to have. For the expression quoted by Eusebius from Agrippa Castor, that Basilides wrote twenty-four books[70] " on the Gospel," almost compels us to turn our thoughts to those Gospels which, according to that earliest form of speech which comes to light even in Justin and Irenæus, were designated as "the Gospel," even although the Gospel of the Hebrews, passing under the name of Matthew, was the substitute for our Matthew. That this view of the work of Basilides, on the skeptical side, is simply ludicrous, may be seen at a glance. Still it is in harmony with what we gather from the letters of Ignatius, from Polycarp, and from Jus-

tin, respecting the place which the Gospels
held in the first half of the second century.
The fragments which have been alluded to do
not invalidate this view, but rather confirm it.
So, too, what Clemens cites (Strom. 3: 1) as
from Basilides is closely connected with Matt.
xix. 11, 12;[71] the quotation from Basilides,
found in Epiphanius (Hær. 24: 5), is in direct
alliance with Matt. vii. 6 ;[72] that found in Origen in the commentary (lib. v. cap. 5) to the
Epistle to the Romans begins with the words
from Romans vii. 9 ; his words are, " For the
apostle has said, ' Once I lived without the
law.' " From this we infer the general connection of Basilides with our New Testament.[73]

To this must be added what we learn through
the Philosophumena of Hippolytus concerning
Basilides. This work contains a detailed account of him, having direct quotations from
Paul[74] and Luke,[75] an allusion to Matthew, and
two passages from John. In vii. 22, we read,
" And that is what is said in the Gospels, ' He
was the true Light, which lighteth every man
that cometh into the world.' " John i 9.

In this passage the expression " in the Gospels" is entitled to its due weight : it presupposes the existence of the evangelical canon hinted at in the other forms of quotation, such as " the Scripture says," and " it is written." Furthermore, in vii. 27, we find the expression " That everything has its time " is amply confirmed by the words of the Saviour, when he says, " My hour is not yet come." John ii. 4. Does not this bring into perplexity those who are so certain that at the time of Basilides not a word of John's Gospel was written ? But no; there is a ready way out of this difficulty. That to which the words, " in the Gospel it is said," give a happy indication, is made to mean, (because, forsooth, no trace of a collection of Gospels can be traced back to that epoch,) that Hippolytus is not dealing with the genuine Basilides, but with a Basilidian document which was the product of his own time. Without entering upon an investigation of that discrimination which Hippolytus, who is so familiar with all that pertains to the ancient heretics, has made between his Basilides and the one yet

7

more ancient, we must at least grant that he
has made distinct and explicit [76] reference to
the older Basilides, and that he is not satisfied
with his reader's accepting any other.   Are we
to suppose that it was a simple matter for the
man who had been the disciple of Irenæus, and
had died in the year 235, to err so singularly,
while in the latest years of his life he was preparing a work drawn from first sources, as
to ascribe to Basilides at the time of Hadrian
what had been added during his own time by
the followers of Basilides ?   Are we able to determine with certainty when the old system left
off and the new began ?   And if we deny them
both, and dare give credence to Hippolytus, we
must admit that he has done us a great service
in showing conclusively that Basilides and his
school recognized the Gospels as books of ecclesiastical authority long before the middle of the
second century, and expressly made use of the
Gospel of John for his ends.

We come to the same result if we trace the
relations of other Gnostic sects, the Naasenians
and the Perates for example.   The first derive

their name from the Hebrew word *naas*, a snake,
corresponding to the Greek Ophites. While the
last name was long used by Irenæus and others,
that of Naasenians began to be made current
(aside from reference of Theodoret) [77] through
the Philosophumena of Hippolytus. That the
Naasenians were nothing but a fraction of the
Ophites is not at all substantiated by the efforts
made to support this hypothesis, and is wholly
disproved by the statement of Hippolytus, who
put the Naasenians and the Perates at the
head of the Gnostics, giving them precedence
before Simon Magus, the Valentinians, and
Basilides, but, as he states expressly (v. 6), assigning them priority over all the other Gnostics. But while we place the opinion of Hippolytus above the doubts which negative criticism has raised, we yet reckon among the most
valuable comments on the Gospels the following
excerpts made by Hippolytus from the writings
of the Naasenians living in the first half of the
second century. In v. 8 he has this : " For all
things, he asserts, (the writer of the Naasenian
document) have been made by the same hand,

and without that hand is nothing made. And
what is made in him [78] is Life." [79]   In another
passage : " That it is which we have learned
of the Saviour, ' Except ye drink my blood and
eat my flesh, ye shall not enter the kingdom of
heaven (John vi. 53) ; Except ye drink the cup
which I drink (Mark x. 38 ; Matt. xx. 22) ;
Whither I go ye can not come.' "   John viii.
21.   Soon after he says, " His voice we have
heard indeed, but his form have we not seen."
John iii. 8 ; v. 37.   In the same connection
we find, " Touching this our Saviour says, ' No
man can come to me except my heavenly
Father draw him.' "   John vi. 44.   Again, v. 9,
" For, says he, God is a Spirit, and those who
worship him must worship him neither on this
mountain nor in Jerusalem, but in spirit."
Cf. John iv. 21, 24.   Soon after we meet the
words, " But if thou knewest who it is that asks
thee, thou wouldest have asked of him, and he
would have given thee living water."   Connected with these passages, so evidently from John,
there are others from Matthew (vii. 6, 13, 14 ;

iii. 10 ; xiii. 3, et sq.), and from Paul's Epistles
(1 Cor. ii. 13, 14 ; 2 Cor. xii. 2, et sq.)

We ought not to refrain from adding to these
Naasenian citations from John and found in
Hippolytus, what is given to us in the writings
of the Ophites, in that pseudo-Tertullianic document (Append. to Text de præscr. hæret.)
which those who lean to the Philosophumena
believe to be drawn from a writing still more
ancient. The quotation from John stands in
the closest relation to that glorification of the
serpent from which the sect of Naasenians derives its name ; and all the more forcibly are
we compelled to assign to the founder of the
sect, and not to some later effort from it, the
application of the passage from John. In the
pseudo-Tertullian (chap. 47 of the document
de præscr. hær.) it is expressly stated, " To
these must be added those heresiarchs who are
called Ophites, i. e., Serpent-men. These pay
such honors to the serpent that they place it
even before Christ. For to the serpent, they
say, we owe the beginning of our knowledge of
good and evil. When Moses comprehended

the greatness and power of the serpent, he elevated one of brass, and all who looked upon it
were made whole.   Besides this, they assert
that even Christ hints at the sacredness of the
serpent, when he says, ' And as Moses lifted up
the serpent in the wilderness, even so must the
Son of man be lifted up.' "   John iii. 14.   We
meet the same passage, as I shall presently
show, in the literature of the Perates.   For just
as from the writings of the Naasenians many
passages were selected by Hippolytus, so were
many also taken from those of the Perates,
especially such as were originally derived from
the Gospel of John.   I need cite but two of these,
Art. v. 12.   " For the Son of man is not come
into the world to condemn the world, but that
through him the world might be saved."   John
iii. 17 ; v. 16.   " And as Moses lifted up the
serpent in the wilderness, even so must the Son
of man also be lifted up."   John iii. 14.[80]

I have as yet made no mention of Marcion, a
man whose nature and activities were strangely
divided between the faith of the church and the
Gnostic heresy.   It is the more necessary for me

to allude to him because use has been made of
his writings in a way entirely at variance with
my own convictions. He was born at Sinope,
on the Black Sea, the celebrated Pontine capital of that time, in the early part of the second
century. Subsequently to the year 128 he appears to have inculcated his peculiar doctrines
at Rome ; and, making it his special purpose to
sever Judaism from Christianity, he undertook
to eliminate from the apostolic writings everything which favored the former. In consequence of a statement which has come down to
us from antiquity, that this writer made a collection of sacred writings (which may have
taken place before the middle of the second
century, between 130 and 140),[81] and that he
admitted into this collection only the Gospel
of Luke and ten of Paul's Epistles, making such
changes, moreover, in the text of them all as
compelled them to suit his ideas, many scholars
have supposed that this was the very first collection of sacred writings made by the church,
and that the Gospel which he admitted into
his collection was not Luke's, but was the

model which was followed when the one which
we possess and call Luke's Gospel was written,
and that he had no acquaintance with our other
Gospels, including that ascribed to John.

All three of these positions we hold to be
utterly untenable. The first of them, which
gives to Marcion the priority in making a collection of New Testament Scriptures for the
use of the church, rests upon a complete ignoring of the development of the canon ; the elements of this development, as my own researches reveal them, I shall take occasion to
sum up and present on a future page. It also
rests upon an ignoring of the point of view which
Marcion took in relation to the church. Taking his stand upon the ground of Paul's expressions in the second chapter of the Epistle to the
Galatians respecting those departures from the
purity of the faith which were beginning to be
manifested among the apostles themselves, he
believed himself called, in the Pauline sense of
the word, to the task of purging the Christian
faith of Jewish elements.[82] In executing this
undertaking nothing was more effective than

the laying of a correcting hand upon those
writings which even then were accepted as the
valid standards of belief among the adherents
of Christianity. The correctness of this mode
of procedure, employed even by the oldest
fathers of the church, was confirmed in a striking manner in his dealing with the Pauline
Gospels. It is confirmed, moreover, by his treatment of Luke's Gospel, of which I shall have
occasion to speak further on. And does it not
harmonize entirely with his purpose, that he excluded other New Testament writings from his
canon? It is possible that in one or another
of the excluded documents the same anti-judai-
cal spirit would have led to like results; yet it
is perfectly conceivable, and is not open to our
criticism, that in his devotion to Paul he contented himself with accepting ten of his Epistles
and that Gospel, whose author, owing to his
being a companion and helper of Paul, owed
a great deal to the influence exerted upon him
by Paul, so that his work might almost be
called the Gospel according to Paul.[83]

Very recently[84] the statement has been made

with consummate *naïveté*, that Marcion, so-
journing in a remote province like Pontus, enjoyed a limited accessibility to Christian books,
and that in making his collection he accumu-
lated the greatest amount of materials that his
scanty advantages allowed.   The distance of
that province, which at the time of Pliny com-
prised a very large population of Jews as well
as of Christians, from the two centers of
Christian Asia Minor, Ephesus and Antioch, is
not greater than from Naples to Milan; and
who in all the world, except a short-sighted
professor, would draw the inference that a
scholar, living in Pontus, during the fourth
decade of the second century, making a collection of the Christian sacred books, was not acquainted with all our Gospels?   The Epistles
to the Corinthians and to the Romans were
diffused and accepted; and yet we are to believe that the Gospel of John had not found
its way from Ephesus to Sinope![85]   Finally, the
theory which rests on the remoteness of Pontus loses all its force in helping us solve the
question under discussion, from the fact that

after Marcion went to Rome, and took a high
position there, he did not modify at all what
he had done in forming his collection of sacred
writings. At Rome he would assuredly have
been able to supply the lack of materials from
which he is alleged to have suffered at Pontus ;
but we do not learn that he made any addition
to his canon after coming to Rome.

The second of the positions mentioned above,
that the gospel of Marcion served as a model
for that which we now accept as Luke's — a
position which bears the clearest evidence from
the outset of being the result of reckless ignorance — has been surrendered in our own time by
its own defenders.   Still it is asserted by some
scholars that our Gospel according to Luke,
like that of Marcion, is a modified form of one
still older but subsequently lost; that that of
Marcion consequently did not spring from
Luke's, but that they both originated in a common source, to which Marcion remained true.
Going in this direction one step further, they
succeeded in finding in Marcion the oldest of all
the Gospel Codices.   This view, entirely apart

from the last mentioned bold act of an intoxi-
cated fancy, is in opposition to what Irenæus,
Tertullian, and Epiphanius say [86] regarding Marcion's gospel, which they possessed ; in consequence, however, of the ignorance prevailing respecting Marcion's labors, and in consequence
also of some indemonstrable hypotheses, it has
gained a certain appearance of truth and conse-
quent acceptance.   The efforts to strike out the
subsequent additions from our Gospel of Luke
for the purpose of restoring the supposed older
original, suffer from that arbitrariness which
modern hypercriticism has assumed in all discussion of the origin of the Gospels.   The fact
that Marcion gave no name [87] to his Gospel is
made to give support to the claim that it is the
only true Gospel, and is entitled to no influence in directing our researches respecting this
Gospel.

We come to the third position, a refutation of
which will throw light upon both of the others.
Marcion is asserted to have not possessed the
other Gospels, including that of John.   If Marcion found the other Gospels in their main

form, just as we possess them now, in the possession of the church of his time, the view of
the priority of his collection over the primitive
canon of the church falls to the ground ; and
equally frail is the hypothesis respecting the
parallelism between the Gospel according to
Marcion and our Luke, together with the con-
sequences drawn therefrom respecting the authority of our canon in its present form ; and
so there is gained no insignificant proof of the
high antiquity and the genuineness of the Gospel according to John.

What grounds have we for believing that
Marcion was acquainted with our Gospels ?
All that Irenæus and Tertullian still more explicitly have told us in reference to this matter
makes it certain. For where Irenæus (i. 27,
2) writes concerning Marcion, that in opposition to his pupils he held his trustworthiness greater than that of the apostles, who
transmitted the Gospel (qui evangelium tradi-
derunt), inasmuch as he did not give the (whole)
Gospel, but a part of the Gospel (non evangelium, sed particulam evangelii), the meaning is,

according to Irenæus's use of language elsewhere (i. 27, 2), that Marcion gave his disciples
only one of the Gospels, namely, that of Luke.
That by the expressions "evangelium" and
"particulam evangelii" we are to understand
the Gospels, and not the Sermon on the Mount,
is shown by another passage of his work (iii. 12,
12), where, in reference to Marcion and other
heresiarchs, we read, " The apostles have spread
the Gospel abroad filled with Jewish prejudices
(adhuc quæ sunt Judæorum sentientes): and
these are even more fair and wise than the
apostles." Irenæus then goes on to say, " On
this account Marcion and his adherents have
made it their aim to diminish the extent of the
sacred books (ad intercidendas scripturas conversi sunt), some of which they have entirely
rejected, while they have reduced the size of
Luke's Gospel and Paul's Epistles, insisting
that the scriptures which they have retained
and revised are the only ones which are to be
accepted." These statements of Irenæus have
no twofold meaning, and are not susceptible of
two interpretations. He evidently presupposes

a familiar knowledge on the part of the reader of what he means by the "reducing of the sacred books," and by a "non-recognition" of some of them : and in order to understand what he means we have only to take his own point of view.

Tertullian's admissions are much more to the purpose, although in his case we have to bear in mind that he is not writing for critical scholars, who are accustomed to avail themselves of every lack in a complete chain of evidence to help support their own views. After citing (adv. Marc. iv. 3) Marcion's misuse of the second chapter of the Epistle to the Galatians (see a previous page), he says: "Connititur ad destruendum statum eorum evangeliorum quæ propria et sub apostolorum nomine eduntur vel etiam apostolicorum, ut scilicet fidem quam illis adimit suo conferat." Among the Gospels which he designates as those "which bear the name of apostles, or men of apostolic character," are to be understood the four which we possess, unless we purposely misinterpret Tertullian's words. Shortly before (iv. 2), he had in the

most definite language [88] designated the Gospels
as books which had been written by actual apostles, such as Matthew and John, as well as by
men of apostolic dignity, such as Mark and
Luke. In order to escape the force of this striking testimony of Tertullian, without accusing
him of ignorance or falsification, an unfortunate
attempt has been made to get rid of the difficulty by asserting that apocryphal Gospels are
here meant, bearing unauthenticated names
of apostles. Whoever listens for an instant to
such a plea — and how one can is hardly to be
imagined — must hold as not genuine the closing words of Tertullian, " and expressly to ascribe to his own testimony the credibility which
he denies to theirs [the apostolic evangelists]."
Tertullian repeats, moreover, respecting the passages from Matthew's Gospel, " Marcion has
stricken this from the Gospel." Comp. adv.
Marc. ii. 17 ; iv. 7. In the passage quoted on
a previous page, de carne Chr. 2, the words,
" tot originalia instrumenta Christi, Marcion,
delere ausus es," are used in direct relation to
the first chapters of Matthew and Luke. Adv.

Marcion iv. 5 he complains of Marcion on the
ground that instead of availing himself of Luke
(a Gospel at second hand), he did not at once
take up those whose authority (as the work of
actual apostles) he knew to be higher.[89] De
carn. Christ. 3, he says, " If thou hadst not purposely rejected or changed the reading of the
writings which are opposed to thy system, the
Gospel of John would surely have convinced
thee in this matter." We find attention called
finally to an epistle of Marcion, from the contents of which Tertullian establishes conclusively the fact that Marcion once accepted what
he subsequently rejected.[90]

From all this it is established with the utmost
certainty that Tertullian subjected Marcion to
weighty reproaches for rejecting the Gospels
(including John, once expressly named) which
he had once accepted, and which Tertullian, in
common with the church, continued to hold.
An epistle of Marcion which he thought might
possibly be disavowed by the followers of Marcion [91] served to show him what was the character of the man. The question naturally comes

8

up, Is Tertullian entitled to credibility in this affair ?

It is now difficult to set aside the claims of those who have enacted the history of the primitive Christian church, on a basis of anti-ecclesiastical prejudices and fancies. Polemical zeal, united with a certain passionate force of conviction, sometimes carried the great African polemic too far, and made him unjust to the heretical opponents whom he had to confute. But is this general fact enough to warrant us in crying out that here he is making false inferences? Men have even the hardihood to say — for shamelessness is now an extinct idea — that what Tertullian states with all correctness must be set to the account of " malicious persecution." [92]   That what Tertullian advances finds powerful support in Irenæus is plain ; but when the clearest and most evident matters are made to assume an obscure appearance, how much easier to bring under suspicion the passages from Irenæus, which hint at more than they openly express. Is anything plainer than that the reform [93] which Marcion endeavored to

carry into the Gospels aimed specifically at correcting the canonical writings of the New Testament?   Did Tertullian need the help of
schoolmasters more than we do, to know that
" evangelium " has other meanings than a written record?   And is the accusation brought
against Marcion, that he rejected the apostolic
records, which were well known to him, and
which even bore the authenticated names of
apostles, and that he made arbitrary changes in
Luke as well as in the Pauline Epistles, anything else than empty inference?   And why is
this attempt made?   Is not the object to get
rid of the truth, to undermine and destroy the
force of one of the most important means of
substantiating the primitive authority of our
Gospels, more especially that of John?   Those
readers who are not specially engaged in prose-
cuting learned researches need nothing more
than what has already been given to qualify
them for passing judgment on this matter.
Such readers ought to use every occasion to as-
certian what the character of the learning is,

which those professors sustain who make it their task to decry the authenticity of the Gospels.

One of the most interesting phenomena in the church, and one of lasting influence, was Montanism. Its aim was to stem the violent tide of Gnosticism, which was swamping the simple older faith with philosophic speculation, and sought to benefit men by giving them a deep inward and direct apprehension of divine truth. Taking a stand not only against foreign speculations but equally against the traditional deadness of an external ecclesiasticism, it, like Gnosticism, at length shot above the church through its exaltation of a fanatical spirit of prophecy, above the tranquil and orderly development of Christianity through doctrines of the new birth and spiritual illumination.

If, following the object which I have in view, we ask what place Montanism took in relation to the writings of the New Testament, the greatest difficulty in the way of finding an answer lies in the fact that we are scarcely in a position to make a general discrimination between the form which had been given at the end

of the second century by means of Tertullian's
reformatory character, to the theological system then existing, and that which it had assumed at the outset in Syria. The account
given by Eusebius, although drawn from fragments dating from the comparatively recent time
of Marcus Aurelius (161 to 180), and that of
Epiphanius, which aimed more distinctively at
a confutation of opponents, are of a very incomplete character. The little which Irenæus
has respecting this matter is hinted at in such
various fashion that one hint only darkens the
meaning of another. The scanty allusions in
the Philosophumena of Hippolytus give rise to
the suspicion that they relate rather to Tertullian's epoch than to the beginning of Montanism in the year 150.

The distinctive question which meets us here
is this: Has Montanism from the very first ap-
propriated to itself, independently of John's
Gospel, that prophetic spirit which was poured
out, as is averred, on Montanus, his female companions, and his followers, and which stood in
intimate connection with the Paraclete which

was promised by the Saviour to his disciples
(John xiv. 16, 26) ?   The wanton character of
Phrygian fanaticism leads us to suspect that
the letter of Scripture was held in no regard;
and the extracts quoted in Eusebius (v. 16 to
19), as well as the document of Epiphanius,
contain nothing which can give us any light in
this matter.   It is quite otherwise with what
Eusebius, and, long before him, Irenæus and
Hippolytus record.[94]   In Irenæus (iii. 11, 9)
we read: "But others, in order to do away with
the gift of the Spirit, which, according to the
counsel of the Father, is poured out on all flesh,
do not accept that promise made in the Gospel
of John, that the Lord will send down the Paraclete, casting away not only this prophetic gift,
but the Gospel as well which records its sending.   It is truly their misfortune that, while
granting that there are false prophets, they yet
deny to the church the true and real gift of
prophecy; it is with them as with those who,
because there are hypocrites in the church, withhold themselves from all fraternal converse with
the brethren."[95]   The reference of this passage

to the Montanists we hold in common with
Lucke and others as not at all made out;[96] but
we regard the argument as conclusive, that the
opponents of the Montanists, wittily called by
Epiphanius, in a double use of language, Alogians, are meant. Epiphanius also bears evidence that the Alogians rejected the Gospel
and the Apocalypse of John. But if it is a real
characteristic of the opponents of Montanism,
that they rejected John's Gospel, it is entirely
probable that this was the result of the connection between the prophetic Spirit of the Montanists and the Paraclete of that Gospel. It is not
credible that the Alogians first brought this
connection into view; according to the words
of Irenæus, previously cited, it is certain that he
was already of the opinion that the Alogians
had rejected this Gospel simply because of this
connection, and because it seemed to be drawn
from John. Irenæus may be incorrect in his
supposition that this was the only or the main
ground for the Alogians' rejection [97] of this Gospel; but Epiphanius bears witness that they
could not account for the want of accordance

between John's and the synoptic Gospels. To
me, however, it seems to be necessarily inferred
from the statements of Irenæus that he presupposes that the Montanists themselves brought
their prophetical Spirit into harmony with the
Paraclete of John's Gospel, and therefore made
use of the latter document.   Lastly, we have a
statement of Hippolytus hinted at ; it is found
in the Philosoph. viii. 19, and runs as follows:
" The Phrygian heresiarchs have been infatu-
ated by Priscilla and Maximilla, whom they hold
to be prophetesses because they aver that the
Paraclete has entered into them."

How then lies the matter ? The short extracts given by Eusebius from the writings of
early opponents contain nothing in reference
to the connection between the Montanists'
prophetical Spirit and the Paraclete of John ;
no more do the refutations of Epiphanius ; but
Irenæus, Hippolytus, Tertullian,[98] and Eusebius
are united in averring that this connection did
exist; and the fact that the Alogians rejected
the Gospel of John, according to the statement
of Irenæus, assuredly harmonizes with the

honor which was paid by the Montanists to this Gospel.

Yet there has been the same effort to pervert the relation of Montanism to John's Gospel as in the system of Valentine; at least the suspicion has been bruited that that Gospel could only have emanated from the same circle of theological ideas and be the result of the same movement which gave rise to Montanism. What a chaotic confusion of thoughts is there in such a charge as this! what a senseless opposition to John's credibility is betrayed in the effort to pervert and falsify the evidences which go to establish his authenticity! Let us suppose for a minute that John's Gospel sprang into existence like Montanism about the year 150. Despite the fact that the lateness of its appearance must make it seem like the work of a pious fraud, and that in its whole structure and in its details it was unlike the earlier Gospels, the church, no less than those who opposed the church, and especially the Montanists, accepted it with full confidence. To one little sect alone did it fall to raise difficulties between the older

5

Gospel and the more recent one, and in consequence to reject the latter, and yet without
gaining either credit or prominence by the act.
And is it true that there is clear accordance between the Montanist doctrine and that of John's
Gospel? Not in the least. Aside from the
fact that the points where they harmonize relate almost exclusively to the idea of the Paraclete (an idea which appears in the Gospel
without any full development, while in Montanism we are directed rather to the catholicizing notions entertained by Tertullian than
to those held earlier), the divergence between Montanism and John's Gospel is as great
as that between an ecclesiastic prototype and
a heretical copy.

In addition to this, the opponents of Montanism already named give noticeable testimony
against this and similar depreciations of John's
Gospel in the middle of the second century, at
the time of the Montanist movement. They
knew nothing about the story of the Gospel of
John being a new thing first ushered into being in their time; they ascribed both the Gos-

pel and the Apocalypse as unworthy of the church (Epiph. hær. 51, 3) to Corinth, a co-temporary of John.[99] The very opponents of the book, therefore, did not doubt about its age, nor bring it under suspicion; they always ascribed it to the epoch in which John lived. Does not this show that the church had long used that Gospel, and that on that account there was no opening for objections to it on the ground of age? It is to be noticed at the same time that the same heretics consider the Gospel and the Apocalypse as coherent productions, and that they acted as one man in disowning John, and in claiming Corinth as the author. The authorship of the Apocalypse, expressly stated by Justin to be the production of John, has not been doubted even by the Tübingen critics to be the work of John. From the acts of the anti-Montanists, however, it is to be inferred that the conviction and usage of the church agreed in ascribing both writings, the Gospel and the Apocalypse, to John.

In this way, as the reader can perceive, even the heretics of the first half of the second century and the beginning of the second half do good service in helping us ascertain the truth regarding the antiquity of our Gospels. We hold it impossible, without resorting to sophistry and falsification, to do away with the testimony which these heretics bear to the credibility of our Gospels, and especially to that of John.

We now advance a step beyond the church to the territory where we encounter the armed opponents of Christianity, the men to whom the whole preaching of the cross was folly and an offense. At that very time when the Gnostic errorists were throwing the church into into such confusion, it happened that one of these opponents, Celsus by name, wrote a book full of mockery and scorn at Christianity. This production perished long ago ; but so far from doing any harm to Christianity, it proved to be a great gain, for it impelled Origen to write his powerful and learned defense of Christianity. From Origen's work we draw enough to make us certain that in his attacks on the Christian faith Celsus made ample use of our Gospels, and that he drew from them the mate-

rials which he needed in making his attacks.
In what he says respecting the appearance of
angels at the resurrection of Jesus he probably
refers to all four of the Gospels; for he says
that according to some there were two angels,
according to others, four at the grave (5, 56).
Origen supposed that the first referred to Luke
and John, the last to Matthew and Mark. Proceeding in a different and more definite way to
work, he drew into the circle of his criticism
various passages from the synoptical Gospels,
especially Matthew's, and also some from that
of John. Among those from the synoptical Gospels may be mentioned the account of the wise
men from the East (whom he calls Chaldeans),
the story of the slaughter of the children by
Herod (1, 58), the flight into Egypt at the bid-
ding of the angel (1, 66), the appearance of the
dove at the baptism (1, 40), the son of the Virgin (1, 40), the direction which Jesus gives to
his disciples (Matt. x. 23), "when they perse-
cute you in this city, flee ye into another " (1,
65), the grief at Gethsemane (2, 24), the thirst
on the cross (2, 37), the saying of Jesus that it

is easier to go through the eye of a needle, etc.
— which he supposes to be a motto of Plato in a
changed form (6, 16),—the command of Jesus
(Matt. v. 39 ; Luke vi. 29), " Whosoever shall
smite thee on thy right cheek, turn to him the
other also," which he also supposes to be a modified Platonism.   Examples of a reference to John
are, his statement (1, 67) that the Jews in the
temple demanded a sign of Jesus (John ii. 18),
that he accepts John's expression " Logos" to
designate Jesus as the Word of God (2, 31), that
he ridicules (2, 36) the statement that at the
crucifixion blood issued from Jesus' side (John
xix. 34), and that he asserts (2, 59) that after
his resurrection Jesus displayed his pierced
hands as the token of what he had endured
(John xx. 27).   It can not be claimed, in view
of this, that Celsus drew all these assertions from
living Christian tradition ; for he himself is the
very one to lay stress upon the fact that he
drew upon the writings of the Christians.   His
words were, as cited literally by Origen (2, 74),
from his own writings : " And this we have
drawn from your own books; we want no fur-

ther evidence, and you are impaled on your
own sword." Origen remarks appositely that
Celsus has indeed brought forward much that
was not in the Gospels, especially some blasphemous reports about Mary, and some idle stories
about the infancy of Christ; these may be found
alluded to in the first book which Origen wrote
contra Celsum[100] (1, 28 and 32). But in
the course of his work Celsus carried out his
idea[101] of adhering closely to the " writings of
the disciples of Jesus." And plainly this was
done out of respect to the fact that these writings, and these alone, had authority in the
church.

The question here arises, What relation to the
witness which Celsus bears to the authority of
our Gospels is sustained by that criticism which
does not accept that authority, so far especially
as John is concerned ? As that evidence can
not be impugned, unbelieving scholars bring
into use again here that modernizing system
which crops into view in Herakleon, to the perfect shame of him who first made it current.
As in Herakleon, so here, the story runs, Celsus

was the cotemporary of Origen. But when was
that important fact ascertained? Drawing
from Origen himself, Dr. Volkmar [102] says, "Has
not Origen declared at the close of his work
(8, 76) that the same Celsus announced that he
would publish a work of more positive character, and that we must wait to see whether he
would accomplish the undertaking? Origen
(254) may have written his book against Celsus
about the middle of the first half of the third
century. Nothing is plainer than that Cel
sus, if he were alive at that time and giving
men to understand that a new work might be
expected from his pen, has no importance to us
in helping us settle this matter. But even here
we have to deal with nothing but a piece of
wretched trickery, with real poverty of resources
on the part of the critics whom I complain of.
For the statement borrowed from the close of the
work against Celsus rests upon gross ignorance
or upon purposed deception. The words of
Origen to his patron Ambrosius, who had stim-
ulated him to write the whole Apology, run
after this wise: " Know that Celsus promised

[unquestionably in his book directed against
Christianity, and opposed by Origen] to write
still another work in which " . . . . " If now
he has not written this, in spite of his promise [103]
it is enough for us to answer him with these
eight books. But if he has done this, and com-
pleted [104] his later work, do you hunt it up and
send it to me, that I may answer it," etc. The
difficulty to account for is in the words, "we
must wait to see whether he would accomplish
the undertaking." But at the outset, in the
very first book, Origen says, " I do not know of
a single Christian whose faith is in peril of being endangered by Celsus, a man no longer
among the living, but who has been a long
time numbered among the dead." They for-
got, of course, to cut out this passage with the
scissors which had been so effectually applied
to Polycarp. In that same first book Origen
says, " We have learned that there have been
two men bearing the name of Celsus, the first
under Nero, the second [i. e. ours] under Hadrian and later." It is not impossible that
Origen erred in identifying his Celsus with the

Epicurean who lived "under Hadrian. and later;" but it is impossible to make the Celsus of
whom Origen thus speaks, his cotemporary.
Could Origen have made Celsus in his first book
to be "under Hadrian and later" (117 to 138),
and in the eighth have said of the same man, "we
must wait to see [about 225] whether he will
accomplish his undertaking?" So long therefore as we get no more reliable information respecting Celsus, we must remain content with
believing that he wrote his work about the middle of the second century, perhaps between 150
and 160 ;[105] and that his testimony in favor of
the synoptic and Johannean Gospels dates from
that period, — a fact of very great weight in enabling us to determine the early existence of
the evangelical canon.

With this result, however, we by no means
reach the limits of the history of Apologies for
the Gospels. In order to complete this depart-
ment of our subject, we now enter upon a peculiar branch of the literature of the same age
with that with which we have been dealing, —
a branch which, after long neglect, is in our

day claiming new and respectful attention;
viz., the New Testament apocryphal literature.
This holds a certain position midway between
the literature of the church and that of the
heresiarchs: at any rate, many of its features
served the ends of the former through the use
of the latter. It is necessary, however, that I
should instruct the reader what the theologians
understand by the term " apocrypha." The
apocryphal writings of the New Testament — for
it is of these only that I speak — are writings
which aimed to take their place on the same
footing with the writings of the New Testament, but which were rejected by the church.
They bore on the face of them the names of
apostles, or of other eminent men; but these
names have been misappropriated by unknown
writers for the purpose of recommending what
they wrote. The Apocrypha were written, partly
in order to develop in arbitrary fashion what
their authors had drawn from Scripture, partly
to incorporate unauthenticated accounts of the
Saviour, Mary, Joseph, and the apostles, and
partly to give point and efficacy to heretical

opinions directed against Holy Writ. The church was warranted, therefore, in excluding them from her accepted writings. It is true that they have been revered as authentic by many from the earliest times ; and on this account they have a varied interest[106] to readers. I have indicated elsewhere in what sense I propose to use them : they only support and strengthen our evidence of the very early origin of our Gospels. We are, of course, independent of the question how old the apocrypha are ; and this has left an opening into which opponents have pressed, hoping to cut us off on this side. But we have come to the result that the two portions of the apocryphal Gospels which are extant now, known as the Protevangel of James and the Acts of Pilate, must have been written within the three first decades of the second century, and that the main substance of those works (though marred by many changes in the text) is now in our possession.

The chief, if not the only, evidence for the age of both of these writings is found in Justin. And first with regard to the Protevangel of

James. In Justin's Dialogue with the Jew
Tryphon, and in his first Apology, we find in
the statements respecting the birth of Jesus
and the annunciation traces of a knowledge,
and of the influence, of the book of James.
Justin relates in the Dialogue (cap. 78) that
the birth of Jesus occurred in a cavern near
the village, there being no room at the inn.
This statement, which confirms the account of
Luke instead of contradicting it, is contained
in the book of James, and is woven into the
substance of the whole history of the event.
Still, it is not to be overlooked that Justin
appropriates only this single fragment respecting the birth in the cave, and in the rest follows Luke rather than the pseudo-James. The
statement respecting the want of room in Beth-
lehem coheres strictly with the narrative of
Luke, but is not in accord with that of the
pseudo-James. Similarly, the annunciation is
plainly hinted in the first Apology, although
with a free following of Luke, with the mere
difference that the words, " For he shall save
his people from their sins," are connected with

the words directed to Mary, " And thou shalt
call his name Jesus." In Luke they are wanting altogether, and in Matthew they belong to
the message announced to Joseph. And have
we not a recognition of what is apocryphal in
Justin, since, at the close of his exposition, he
appeals to those who have declared everything
respecting our Saviour Jesus Christ ? But no,
that can not be said; for the whole account
of Justin, as already remarked, corresponds
strictly to Luke, and not to the Protevangel,
only with this difference, that the passage indicated varies from the Protevangel, Matthew
giving the words as announced to Joseph, and
Justin as addressed to Mary. This feature
must, in my opinion, be ascribed to the perusal
of the Protevangel; and in the recollection of
Justin it connected itself with Luke's account
without his own consciousness of the fact. It
is unmistakable that the whole quotation was
made from memory.[107] In the Dialogue (chap.
100), the annunciation made to Mary is cited,
and the words spring from Luke, and not from
the Protevangel.[108] At the same time, there is

a single extract bearing relation to the mental
state of Mary, which seems to have sprung
from a recollection of a passage in the Protevangel; only Justin has connected it with the
reply of Mary to the address of the angel, while
the Protevangel joins it to a priestly blessing
which she received just on the point of setting
out to visit Elizabeth.[109]

But is there no objection urged against our
endeavor to substantiate an acquaintance of
Justin with the Protevangel? Certainly there
are lost writings which are brought into requi-
sition. Out of one of these it is supposed that
Justin can just as well have drawn as that the
Protevangel be derived from it. The Gnostic
γέννα Μαρίας (de generatione Mariæ), and still
more the Gospel of Peter,[110] have been thought
to be that ancient work freshly brought to
light. And this brings us into renewed contact
with an old acquaintance, with that same fac-
ulty of making new discoveries of which I have
already had occasion to speak. In order to
escape the force of a work lying plainly before
our eyes, the inferences from which are un-

mistakable, it is held in the light of a copy of a perished work, of which we have received from the past little but the title and a few meager extracts, which render it impossible to set solid facts over against the play of fancy. Yet let us look into this matter as closely as we can. Epiphanius [111] has given the first impulse toward bringing the Gnostic production already mentioned into relation with the Protevangel, in citing something of what he calls the " shocking " statements of the work; namely, that there appeared to Zacharias in the temple the vision of a man wearing the form of an ass. Upon which Zacharias went up to him and tried to say, Woe to you! whom are you worshiping? but could not utter the words, the man seen in the vision having struck him dumb. But when his mouth was opened, and he had communicated to others what he had seen, he was instantly put to death. This fragment from the lost book is enough, I should think, to identify its source. And is there that in it which enables us to determine that it was the basis of the Protevangel? The last has noth-

ing in common with the first, excepting the
slaughter of Zacharias, but wholly on another
ground, and under altogether different condi-
tions. But there is help at hand against accu-
mulating difficulties respecting the connection
of both writings. The way is to conjure up
and thrust into prominence a work which
claims to have given rise to that of James.
From the Gnostic book relating to Mary sprang
this Gnostic-tinged — now unfortunately lost —
primitive foundation of the pseudo-James; and
from this again the work of our catholicizing
James.[112] This ingenious solution may not
have quite satisfied even him who hit upon it,
and hence he thought out and gave preference
to another combination. In the passage where
Origen alludes to the work of James, he mentions the Gospel of Peter; for he says the
brothers of Jesus were regarded by some, who
followed the tradition of the Gospel of Peter,
or that of James's work, as if they had been
the sons of Joseph by a previous marriage.[113]
Now, according to this new combination, the
question is asked, Can not the Gospel of Peter,

or the early history given in it, be the basis of
the Protevangel?   The primitive history in the
Gospel of Peter rests exclusively upon the passage of Origen relating to the brothers of Jesus
as the sons of Joseph by an earlier marriage
With reference to this, we read without going
further.   That there was such a primitive history, can, according to the statement of Origen,
be regarded as beyond doubt.   From the same
passage of Origen, the conclusion is drawn that
"in the Protevangel of James the primitive history of the Gospel of Peter is contained."   But
do the words of Origen, "while they followed
the tradition of the Gospel of Peter, or that of
the work of James," warrant the inference in
the least that the latter coincides and gives
support to the primitive history of the Gospel
of Peter?   But who is able to impose a check
upon the unbridled fanaticism of theorists?[114]
That we are now in possession of nearly fifty
Greek manuscripts, comprising, among other
things, a Syrian copy of the work under discussion, dating from the sixth century, and that
no one of the evidences of its antiquity, from

Origen down, is contradictory to the text of these manuscripts, gives us assuredly a good right to hold fast to the conviction that this was the writing so familiar to the ancients,[115] and so much used by them. Is not that the most untenable of hypotheses, that our work was derived from one which was used by the ancients where it coincides with our own, but of which not a trace remains? And what other end does this hypothesis subserve than this, to set aside the inferences which are drawn from the book of James, and applied not only to the Christian literature of the second century, but more especially to the history of the Gospel cause? I trust it will not impel those who do not share these views, to regard hypotheses which have such a basis to rest upon as something else than they really are. In opposition to them, I am still justified in insisting that the undeniable connection between Justin and several passages of the so-called Proto-Gospel presupposes his acquaintance with this very production. The book of James stands, in its whole tendency, in such a relation to our

canonical Gospels, that the latter must have
been diffused a long time, and must have been
accepted a long time before the former was discovered. The allusions of Matthew and Luke
to the virgin mother of the Lord were unable
to prevent the belief in a real son of Joseph
and Mary, — an idea consonant with the taste of
the Judaized Christian heresiarchs : the mention of the brothers of Jesus in the synoptic
Gospels appeared to bear evidence against Matthew and Luke ; learned Jews brought against
the Christians the charge of arbitrarily chang-
ing the meaning of Isaiah, and making him
support the notion of a virgin mother : Jewish
hostility even went so far as to assert that Jesus
was the illegitimate son of one Panthera, and
heathen skeptics quoted Greek fables about
sons being born from virgins, in order to discredit the evangelical account. In such a time
as was the first half of the second century,
nothing could promise a better support to the
Gospel narrative than a production like the one
named after James, furnished with irrefragable
historic testimony as to the lofty destiny of

Mary from her birth, as to her motherhood
while a virgin, and as to a relationship of Mary
to Joseph exalted far above the usual relations
of marriage.[116] Now, if this work of James
falls within the first three decades of the second century, the composition of the Gospels of
Matthew and Luke, to which the reference of
James's work limits itself, can not be set later
than the last decades of the previous century.

It is the same with the second apocryphal
work brought under review above, the so-called
Acts of Pilate, only with the difference that
they refer as much to John as to the synoptical
Gospels. Justin, in like manner as before, is
the most ancient voucher for this work, which
is said to have been written under Pilate's
jurisdiction, and, by reason of its specification
of wonderful occurrences before, during, and
after the crucifixion, to have borne strong evidence to the divinity of Christ. Justin saw as
little reason as Tertullian and others for believing that it was a work of pious deception from
a Christian hand. On the contrary, Justin
appeals twice to it in his first Apology in order

to confirm the accounts of the occurrences
which took place at the crucifixion in accordance with prophecy, and of the miraculous
healings effected by Christ, also the subject of
prophetic announcement. He cites specifically
(chap. 35) from Isaiah lxv. 2, and lviii. 2: " I
have spread out my hands all the day unto a
rebellious people, which walketh in a way that
was not good." . . . " They ask of me the
ordinances of justice: they take delight in ap-
proaching to God. Further, from the twenty-
second Psalm: "They pierced my hands and my
feet. . . . They parted my garments upon
them, and cast lots upon my vesture." With
reference to this, he remarks that Christ fulfilled
this; that he did stretch forth his hands when
the Jews crucified him, — the men who contended against him, and denied that he was the
Christ. " Then," he says further, " as the
prophet foretold, they dragged him to the judg-
ment-seat, set him upon it, and said, ' Judge us.'
The expression, however, ' they pierced,' etc.,
refers to the nails with which they fastened his
hands and his feet to the cross. And after they

had crucified him they threw lots for his clothing, and they who had taken part in the act of
crucifixion divided it among themselves." To
this he adds: " And you can learn from the
Acts, composed [117] during the governorship of
Pontius Pilate, that these things really happened." Still more explicit is the testimony
of Tertullian. It may be found in the Apolo-
geticus (chap. 2), where he says that out of
envy Jesus was surrendered to Pilate by the
Jewish ceremonial lawyers, and by him, after
he had yielded to the cries of the people, given
over for crucifixion ; that while hanging on the
cross he gave up the ghost with a loud cry, and
so anticipated the executioner's duty ; that at
that same hour the day was interrupted by a
sudden darkness ; that a guard of soldiers was
set at the grave for the purpose of preventing
his disciples stealing his body, since he had
predicted his resurrection, but that on the third
day the ground was suddenly shaken, and the
stone rolled away from before the sepulcher ;
that in the grave nothing was found but the
articles used in his burial ; that the report was

spread abroad by those who stood outside, that
the disciples had taken the body away; that
Jesus spent forty days with them in Galilee,
teaching them what their mission should be,
and that, after giving them their instructions
as to what they should preach, he was raised
in a cloud to heaven. Tertullian closes this
account with the words, " All this was reported
to the emperor at that time, Tiberius, by Pilate, his conscience having compelled even him
to become a Christian."

The document now in our possession corresponds with this evidence of Justin and Tertullian. Even in the title it agrees with the account of Justin, although, instead of the word
acta, which he used, and which is manifestly
much more Latin than Greek, a Greek expression is employed, which can be shown to have
been used to indicate genuine Acts.[118] The
details recounted by Justin and Tertullian are
all found in our text of the Acts of Pilate, with
this variation, that nothing corresponds to what
is joined to the declaration of the prophet,
" They dragged him to the seat of judgment,

and set him upon it, and said," etc. : besides
this, the casting lots for the vesture is expressed
simply by the allusion to the division of the
clothes. We must give even closer scrutiny to
one point. Justin alludes to the miracles
which were performed in fulfillment of Old Testament prophecy, on the lame, the dumb, the
blind, the dead, and on lepers. In fact, in our
Acts of Pilate there are made to appear before
the Roman governor a palsied man who had
suffered for thirty-eight years, and was brought
in a bed by young men, and healed on the Sabbath day;[119] a blind man cured by the laying
on of hands ; a cripple who had been restored ;
a leper who had been cleansed ; the woman
whose issue of blood had been stanched ; and
a witness of the raising of Lazarus from the
dead. Of that which Tertullian cites, we will
adduce merely the passage found in no one of
our Gospels, that Jesus passed forty days after
his resurrection in company with his disciples
in Galilee. This is indicated in our Acts of
Pilate, at the end of the fifteenth chapter, where
the risen man is represented as saying to Jo-

seph, " For forty days go not out of thy house ; for behold, I go to my brethren in Galilee."

Every one will perceive how strongly the argument that our Acts of Pilate are the same which Justin and Tertullian read is buttressed by these unexpected coincidences. The assertion recently made [120] requires consequently no labored contradiction that the allusions to both men have grown out of their mere suspicion that there was such a record as the Acts of Pilate, or out of the circulation of a mere story about such a record, while the real work was written as the consequence of these allusions at the close of the third century. What an uncommon fancy it requires in the two men to coincide so perfectly in a single production as is the case in the Acts to which I am now re-ferring! And are we to imagine that they re-ferred with such emphasis as they employed to the mere creations of their fancy ?

The question has been raised with more jus-tice, whether the production in our possession may not have been a copy or free revision of the old and primitive one. The modern change in the title has given support to this conjecture, for it has occasioned the work to be commonly spoken of as the Gospel of Nicodemus. But this title is borne neither by any Greek manuscript, the Coptic-Sahidian papyrus, nor the Latin manuscripts, with the exception of a few of the most recent.[121] It may be traced only subsequently to the twelfth century, although at a very early period, in one of the two prefaces attached to the work, Nicodemus is mentioned in one place as a Hebrew author, and in another as a Greek translator. But aside from the title, the handwriting displays great variation, and the two prefaces alluded to above show clearly the work of two hands. Notwithstanding this, however, there are decisive grounds for holding that our Acts of Pilate contain in its main substance the document drawn from Justin and Tertullian. The first of this to be noticed is, that the Greek text, as given in the version most widely circulated in the manuscripts, is surprisingly corroborated by two documents of the rarest character, and first used by myself, — a Coptic-Sahidian papyrus

manuscript, and a Latin palimpsest, — both probably dating from the fifth century.   Such a documentary confirmation of their text is possessed
by scarcely ten works of the collective Greek
classic literature.   Both of these ancient writings make it in the highest degree probable
that the Egyptian and Latin translations which
they contain were executed still earlier.   But
could a work which was held in great consideration in Justin's and Tertullian's time, and down
to the commencement of the fourth century,
and which strenuously [122] insists that the Emperor Maximin caused other blasphemous Acts of
Pilate to be published and zealously circulated,
manifestly for the purpose of displacing and
discrediting the older Christian Acts, — could
such a work suddenly change its whole form,
and from the fifth century, to which in so extraordinary a manner translators wholly different in character point back with such wonderful concurrence, continue in the new form ?
Contrary as this is to all historical criticism,
there is in the contents of the work, in the singu-
lar manner in which isolated and independent

details [123] are shown to be related to the canonical books, no less than in the accordance
with the earliest quotations found in Justin
and Tertullian,[124] a guaranty of the greatest
antiquity. There are in the contents, also,
matters of such a nature that we must confess
that they are to be traced back to the primitive
edition; as, for example, the narrative in the first
chapter of the bringing forward of the accused.
But the whole character of the work in our possession does not deny in toto that which we
must infer from the statements of Justin and
Tertullian. It is incorrect, moreover, to draw
a conclusion from Justin's designation of the
Acta which is not warranted by the whole character of the work. The Acta, the ὑπομνήματα,
are specified in Justin's account, not less than
in the manuscripts which we possess, as being
written *under* Pontius Pilate; and that can signify nothing else than that they were an official
production, composed under the direct sanction of the Roman Governor. Their transmis-
sion to the Emperor must be imagined as accompanied by a letter of the same character with

that which has been brought down to us in the
Greek and Latin edition,[125] and yet not at all
similar in purport to the notable Acts of Pilate.
It is by no means necessary for us to assert
that the production in our hands has (with the
exception of the preface already alluded to) remained free from interpolations; for the dis-
tinguishing characteristic which it bears is the
weaving in of much from the synoptic Gospels,
and still more from John, relative to the last
sufferings of Jesus.[126]   Is it not stated in Justin that the Acts of Pilate reveal the fulfillment
of the prophecy respecting the resurrection from
the dead, as it is given in chapter eight of
the work in our hands, in the testimony concerning the raising of Lazarus ?   Is it probable
that, in order to set John aside, we are to believe that in Justin's edition there was recorded
one of the two other resurrections, of which we
have traces preserved for us ?

It would lead us to the denial of an unquestionable fact should we not admit the claims of
our Acts of Pilate, in their connection with the
work of the same name known to Justin, to

serve as testimony to the authority of the Johannean as well as the synoptic Gospels, dating
from a period prior to Justin, in spite of their
frequent use of those Gospels. What importance this fact has in enabling us to determine
the age of our Gospels, and especially that of
John, is at once apparent; it weighs far more
than any verbal extracts made from John in
the epoch of Justin. If the apocryphal Acts of
Pilate must, for the reason that Justin cites
them in his first Apology to the Roman Emperor, be ascribed to the first decades of the second
century, they show, by their use of and dependence upon the Gospel of John, that the latter
dates from a period even earlier. This theory
throws no light into the impenetrable darkness,
but, among the many beams which come down
from the period directly after the age of the
apostles, and which illumine the most important question of Christianity, this is one of the
most luminous.

We might also cite Thomas's Gospel of the
Infancy for our purpose. Irenæus and Hippolytus [127] both show that it was used by the Mar-

cosians and the Naasenians; it was therefore unquestionably one of the first results of the pro-
ductive heresy of that age, and must be ascribed
to the middle of the second century. Its text
we possess only in fragments, which are at
issue [128] often among themselves, and which
consequently makes it difficult to ascertain the
connection of scattered passages with those of
the Gospels. The work seems, however, to bear
witness in one respect to the results of my researches, and not in the not unimportant fact
that at the time when this book appeared, in
the middle of the second century, the Gospel
canon ordinarily accepted was already formed,
and the story of the years of Jesus' childhood
filled up a break in the account of his life.
This left a district open to historical research,
and one which heresy knew well how to prize.
Besides this there confronts us one fact more,
which admits of application to the three more or
less perfectly personal evidences of the Christian Apocraphy. The wide divergence found in
these, in respect to form as well as substance, to
language as well as spirit, to delineation as well

as conception, bears witness to a sacred origin
of our canonical Gospels, to which the apocryphal writings are related as the last subjoined
appendices.

I might allude here in a single word to the
pseudo-Clementine literature, whose main work,
the Homilies, is certainly to be ascribed to the
middle of the second century. The establishment of this date does not lead to the necessity
of drawing any such inferences respecting the
history of the canon as we drew in the case of
the book of James and the Acts of Pilate.
Still it is very instructive that the transition of
the Gospel of John into this Judaic-Christian-
tendency record,[129] which was not at all dis-
puted till the year 1853, has been shown to be
utterly untenable by the discovery by Dressel, at
Rome, of the concluding portions of it where
(xix. 22) John's narrative of the man who was
born blind is made use of beyond all doubt.

The elucidation already given respecting the
Acts of Pilate and the book of James had already
brought us to the opening first decades of the
second century, and compelled us to confess

that there was unquestionably use made, at that period, of our Gospels. No one of the remaining results of our investigations into the ecclesiastical and heretical literature of the second century stood in antagonism with this fact. Not only the apocryphal writings already named bring us back to that epoch, but a work of great repute in the Christian literature, one which from even the close of the second century to the opening of the fourth was assigned by such men as Clemens Alexandrinus [130] to Holy Writ. It forms a part of the so-called apostolical Fathers, regarding which we have already spoken in our discussion of the epistles of Ignatius and that of Polycarp. If it really bore rightly the name of Barnabas, the companion of Paul, it would, in spite of certain unsatisfactory details, be correctly entitled to a place among the sacred books of the New Testament. Slight as is the ecclesiastical or scientific recognition granted to this claim of authorship, yet the assertion is made with confidence, that the epistle bearing the name of Barnabas is one of the earliest written records which have

come down to us from the epoch directly subsequent to the life of the apostles. If the expressions (in the sixteenth chapter) conjoined
with the word of prophecy regarding the re-
building of the City and the Temple are in accordance with historical fact, we are brought
back from the conflicting statements respecting
the closing decades of the first century and the
opening decades of the second, to the first year
of Hadrian's reign. In its aim and general
character the epistle bears the closest resemblance, among the books of the New Testament,
to the Epistle to the Hebrews; it is directed
against such Christian converts from Judaism,
who, while accepting the new covenant, sought
to cling to the old, and hence felt that they
must share with the former fellow-believers in
the grief over the fall of the Jewish Temple.
In opposition to them, the epistle, basing itself
largely upon Old Testament prophecy and authority, arrays the proof that the new covenant
brought in by Christ had completely done away
with the older one, and that the latter had
merely been, with its temple and whole service,

an incomplete and temporary type of the new covenant.

Within the last two centuries scholars have busied themselves much with this document, but unfortunately there are lacking in all the Greek manuscripts of it, the first five chapters; only an old Latin translation, greatly incomplete,[131] supplies the deficiency. And exactly in those chapters which are found only in the Latin copy is there a passage which has excited great curiosity. "Let us be on our guard," thus it reads in the fourth chapter, "that we be not be found to be, as it is written, many called but few chosen." "Adtendamus ergo ne forte, sicut scriptum est, multi vocati, pauci electi inveniamur." The expression, "as it is written," will be readily recognized by the reader as a familiar one in the New Testament. It is the phrase which always designates the difference between all passages of Holy Writ and all others, and was invariably used by the apostles, as well as by the Saviour, in citing the Old Testament. If it were ever applied to a passage outside of the canon, it only followed that

the passage in question had been drawn by frequent use into the circle of canonical writings,
just as, for example, Jude cites from the
prophet Enoch. It could be publicly transferred to the writings of the apostles, when the
latter were placed on the same basis with the
Old Testament. As soon as passages of the
Gospels were cited in connection with the
phrase, " as it is written," it was assumed that
they had become canonical. We had occasion
on a former page to allude to this matter, while
referring to Justin's arranging the Gospels and
the Prophecies side by side, and to the epistles
of Ignatius ; the same formula was also encountered in the New Testament quotations of the
Naasenians. The words which have been cited
in the Epistle of Barnabas in connection with
the same formula are in the Gospel of Matthew,
xxii. 14, and xx. 16. If our inference is correct, at the time when the Epistle of Barnabas
was written, this Gospel was regarded as canonical.

But the Epistle of Barnabas extends back to
the highest Christian antiquity. And is it pos-

sible, some ask, that at so remote a period the
passage from Matthew should be marked by
the characteristics of canonization ?   The doubt
conveyed in this question has been materially
strengthened by the circumstance that the passage has hitherto existed only in a Latin form.
It was possible to say, therefore, that this sig-
nificant phrase was added by a translator living long subsequently.   Dr. Credner, in 1832,
wrote these literal words : " The form of citation, sicut Scriptum est, applied to a book of
the New Testament, was wholly without usage
in that time, and not an instance of it can be
found."   The portion of the Epistle of Barnabas which contains the passage under discussion does not exist at present in the original
Greek, but only in a Latin translation.   It was
an easy matter, therefore, for the translator to
subjoin the current formula of quotation ; and
from internal evidence we must accordingly
lay claim to the correctness of the text in the
passage under consideration, till some one shall
show satisfactory proof to the contrary.   In
order to decide the question respecting the an-

tiquity of the formula, it was necessary to con-
sult the original Greek text. It was destined
not to be withheld from the Christian world.
After lying many hundreds of years among the
old parchments at the Convent of St. Catherine
in the wilderness of Sinai, it came to light in a
happy hour; for with the Sinaitic Bible, the
whole of the Epistle of Barnabas was discovered
in the original Greek. And what is the decision which it gives respecting the subject under discussion? It decides that the writer of
the epistle himself placed the important Chris-
tian-classic expression, " as it is written," before
the quotation from Matthew, and that it was
not the work of the translator.

After this important fact was established, a
new question arose, namely, whether important
inferences could be drawn unconditionally from
this phrase. Could not the formula, " as it is
written," be accepted as referring to any book?
How little ground there is for this I have already shown in my explanations of the use to
be made of this formula; and we have no right
to weaken its force in the present instance.

But are we also compelled to recognize its relation to the passage from Matthew? What
would be more evident, if we are to escape the
assaults of unsound and partisan criticism?
A writer of this class has brought forward a
notion which once brought down the scorn of
Credner [132] upon it, namely, that the quotation
of Barnabas's Epistle is to be referred to the
fourth book of Ezra, quoted elsewhere in the
Epistle. [133] There, in the eighth chapter, it is
expressly stated according to the Latin and
Ethiopian text, "nam multi creati sunt (in the
Ethiop., besides, in eo, i. e. mundo) pauci autem
salvabuntur,"—for many have been born, but
few shall be saved. In spite of the applause
which this [134] has received in a certain quarter, it
only shows to what wanton fancies the opposition
brought against the age of our evangelical canon
leads men. The visible absurdity of referring
a citation, taken word for word from Matthew,
to a passage in a book of Ezra, written twenty
years earlier [135] and having quite a different
meaning, is carried so far that the expression
of the Saviour in Matthew is degraded into a

mere " Christian interpretation " of the passage
in Ezra.[136] That Matthew is referred to elsewhere in the Epistle is supposed not to have its
weight in strengthening the citation from him
accompanied by the canonical formula, but to
prove, on the contrary, that Barnabas, with all
his acquaintance with Matthew, did not hold
his work to be a sacred book.[137] It is forgotten
that quite often we meet in the later Fathers,
in connection with direct and express quotations, the same weaving in of a biblical clause
that we have in Barnabas ; and in these cases
the reader is pre-supposed to have that familiarity with Scripture which will enable him to determine what it is which is thus woven in, without its being definitely pointed out with words
or signs of quotation. Thus, for example, in
chapter five of Barnabas's Epistle, we have the
expression, " He chose for his disciples, to go
forth and announce his gospel, men full of sin
and unrighteousness, in order to show that he
had not come to call the righteous, but sinners;
and therefore he revealed himself as the Son of
God." What reader of these words could fail
11

to see in them the reflection of what our Saviour says in Matt. ix. 13, " I am not come to call
the righteous, but sinners to repentance " ? [138]
We have, moreover, in the twelfth chapter,
" Since it is a thing in the future [139] that men
shall say that Christ is David's son, therefore
David himself, comprehending in advance the
error which sinners will make, says, ' The
Lord says unto my Lord, sit thou here on my
right hand until I make thine enemies thy foot-
stool.' " Could Barnabas write this without pre-
supposing that his readers would have Matt.
xxii. 41, et sq. in mind? And in this presupposition is not the recognition of the authority
of the then extant Gospel of Matthew taken for
granted? And if in the same twelfth chapter
of Matthew it is shown how Moses lifted up the
brazen serpent in the wilderness in typification
of the Saviour, " who should suffer (die) and
yet himself give life to others," it is directly
obvious that Barnabas was making use of the
truth hinted at in John iii. 14, even if the
phrase, taken word by word, fails to show this.
It is possible indeed that the writer of this

Epistle wrote independently in this case, as in many others; and yet we are justified in assuming the very great probability that he had the passage of John in mind: still, in assuming this, it by no means follows that his Epistle is written in the same tone as that of John's, and was a reflex of it. The disproportionate number of express quotations from the Old Testament found in Barnabas is in direct relation with the whole character of his Epistle: and no inference can be drawn from it, which invalidates the canonization [140] of the Gospels.

Does, then, the fact indicated by the Epistle of Barnabas, that the Gospel of Matthew was reckoned a part of Holy Writ prior to the year 120, come into hazardous conflict with the results already gained by us in our study of the second century? It is needless to try to answer such a question. There is only downright gain to our side, and that of a new and important link in the chain of proofs supporting the very earliest acceptance of the credibility of the Gospels; a new barrier erected against the idle vagaries of conjecture which have hith-

erto been allowed to float around and hide the
history of the New Testament canon.

But are we compelled to limit to Matthew
the authenticity thus granted to his canonical
value? By no means. All our studies respecting the history of the canon lead to this
result, that the attempt was not made in the
infancy of the church to raise any one of the
Gospels, taken exclusively, to the rank of canonical writings. For we saw, in the first half
of the second century, now Matthew, now John,
now Luke, or one taken in connection with another, come into the foreground; and this
shows conclusively that at that epoch no one
was credited while another was discredited.
The small compass, too, of the literature
which has come down to us from that time,
and the character of the Gospels, taken sep-
arately, — Matthew, for example, being incom-
parably better adapted for quotation than Mark,
— lead to the inference that the one bears witness to the equal worth of the other. And we
learned, too, from Justin's use of the Acts of
Pilate about the year 140, that the Gospel of

John, so much used, not only in those Acts
which were written some few decades before
Justin's Apology, but also in connection with
the synoptic Gospels, must be assigned to the
opening of the second century, Justin himself
having often made use of John, and still more
frequently of Matthew. Is not this alone satisfactory proof that if, at the time when the
Epistle of Barnabas was written, Matthew had
attained to canonical authority, John too must
have had the same ? Basilides used John and
Luke at the time of Hadrian ; Valentin, about
140, John, Matthew, and Luke ; and are there
not safe inferences to be drawn thence that
these writers are in close alliance ?

To this must be added the fact that we so
early and so repeatedly find, as, for example, in
Justin and Agrippa Castor, the separate Gospels united in one whole, and that, in view of
the collective and grand character thus given to
this whole, the name and individuality of each
writer are thrown into the background, but
that, on the other hand, Justin refers occasion-
ally to the discrimination made, at a later day,

by Tertullian, in the character of the four Evangelists, according to which some were the real
disciples of the Lord, and the others apostolical
companions. And how are we to understand
otherwise that soon after the middle of the second century Harmonies of the Four Gospels
were prepared, and that in Irenæus — not to
lose sight of him — the four are unitedly subjected to comment, without the least hint of
there being superior or inferior value on the part
of the separate Gospels? Is there the faintest
indication that, in the course of the second century, the church, while discussing many issues
which are reported to us, took up and passed its
judgment upon the Gospel canon, — a funda-
mental matter; while, before the close of that
century, the same canon meets us everywhere
as having been long accepted?

But when, then, are we to consider that the
canon passed into general acceptance? Everything compels us to assign it to the close of the
first century, or to the opening years of the
second. That was the time when, with the
death of the aged [141] John, all the revered men

who had stood in personal relations with Jesus,
and Paul too, the great apostle to the Gentiles,
had passed away, and could no longer give their
direct authority in all ecclesiastical matters to
the young church; the time when the church
was outgrowing its old home, and stretching
wider and wider out, convulsed within by various movements, and pressed upon without by
hostile assaults, — then it was that men began
to consecrate and regard with hallowing veneration the writings which the founders of the
church had left behind them, gather them up
as imperishable bequests, as well-authenticated
evidences of the life and teachings of the Saviour, the most precious types of what men's
faith and practice should be. The fit time had
evidently come to put these writings on the
same basis as that of the old covenant. The
complete separation of the church from the
synagogue had taken place: subsequently to
the destruction of Jerusalem and of its temple
(about the year 70), the church had been
thrown more decidedly upon itself, and had
become more independent; and it was a signifi-

cant sign of this independence to ascribe to the writings which recorded the life of the Saviour and the deeds of his followers the same sanctity which had long invested the sacred documents of the synagogue, on which Christianity was based.

Do we ask in what way this has taken place? It certainly is not a question which needs much time to enable us to answer it. If men like Matthew, Mark, Luke, and John left on record statements respecting the life of our Lord, who would not have recognized them at once as a precious bequest to the church, and gratefully accepted them? Did it require more than their honored names to insure for their writings the greatest veneration by the whole church? And had not these men all stood in close enough personal relations with the church to insure the latter against receiving any works which should be unauthentic, and palmed off by trickery? And of no Gospel is this more true than of John's. Suppose that it did proceed from the midst of his Asia Minor congregations, and pass into the possession of wider circles; could the least suspicion of a want of genuineness fasten to it? But in case it did not proceed from his own congregations, would the latter not have detected the imposition at once? It was impossible to bring them to accept an unauthentic word of their own bishop; certainly not by deception. But we have the bishop who followed John at Ephesus as one of the witnesses to the authenticity of his Gospel. For if Polycrates, bishop of Ephesus in the last quarter of the second century, in a letter addressed to Victor of Rome (Eus. Hist. Eccl. v. 24), alludes to the apostle buried in Ephesus, and characterized him with the same expression which is used in John xiii. 23 and 25,— " who leaned on the Lord's bosom," — there is beyond all doubt a confirmation of the Gospel. As to the rest, that John was the last who wrote is evidenced not only by the very ancient tradition that he was the one whose name was always mentioned after the others, as we have seen to be the case in the hints drawn from Muratori, in Irenæus, and in the oldest Greek manuscripts,[142] but Clemens Alexandrınus and Eusebius give distinct expression to it in what they have communicated to us respecting the circumstances which gave rise to that Gospel. In the first of these latter writers (see Eus. vi. 14), the wish of friends is represented as prompting the more spiritual-minded disciple to add a fourth Gospel to the other three, for the purpose of recording more distinctly the workings of Jesus' spirit. According to the latter (iii. 24), while confessing the truth and authentic value of the first three Gospels, he is represented as omitting what relates more exclusively to the public activity of Jesus, and giving a needful compliment to the evangelical narrative.

Since, then, the writings left behind by the apostles stand at the very outset in the personal authority of the writers, this authority of course only grew in magnitude after the decease of the persons who have personally been the representatives of the spirit of the Gospel. Out of the vital development of the church grew the primitive canon of the New Testament, and took its place side by side with the Old.

It would be easy to admit that such a canon, in accordance with its evangelical character (not to speak here of its other features), would naturally fall within the time which has been assigned, viz., the close of the first century: this, however, we should not be able to settle definitely [143] unless the history and literature of the whole second proved such a cogent argument in its favor.

There is yet one thing more to add to what has already been said respecting the oldest Christian literature. It is the evidence which Papias gives, and which, more than any other, has been misused by the opponents of our Gospels. The want of positive knowledge which rests upon this man, as well as upon his testimony, makes him not a fit subject to be taken either independently or in antagonism with other witnesses.

From Eusebius (iii. 39) we learn, confirmed as it is by Irenæus (v. 33 : 4), that Papias composed a work in five books, which he called an Exposition of the sayings of our Lord.[144] While he was collecting the materials for this

work he believed that his task was not so
much to cull what was to be found in written
records as in unwritten tradition; and, according to his own assurance, he drew especially
from those oral accounts which could be traced
back to the apostles. These are his own words
regarding his book: " I shall arrange with as-
siduity whatever I may gather from the presbyters (elders), and retain in memory, while
aiming to ascertain the truth of the same by
means of personal investigation. For I did
not find my pleasure, as most do, in those who
have much to tell, but in those who teach the
truth; not in those who bring forward what is
strange, and out of the usual course (τὰς ἀλλο-
τρίας ἐντολάς), but in those who surrender themselves absolutely to the truth,[145] and claim line-
age with what is true. Whenever, therefore, I
fell in with those who used to be on intimate
terms with the presbyters, I made special inquiries as to what Andrew, or Peter, or Philip,
or Thomas, or James, or John, or Matthew, or
any other disciple of the Lord, or as to what Aristion and John the presbyter, disciples also, have

to say.[146] For I believed that the books (τὰ ἐκ τῶν βιβλίων) would not be of so much service to me in giving exhaustive information as the living word of men (quantum ex hominum adhuc superstitum voce)."

This passage of Papias is obscure in various ways, and on this account I have endeavored to translate it literally. The first and most important point to settle is, who the elders or " presbyters " were. Papias alludes to them as his vouchers, whom he used in part directly, in part indirectly. Are the apostles themselves to be regarded as covered by the expression? It is supposed by many that they are; but this notion is absolutely denied and rendered untenable by Eusebius. For, after stating that Irenæus designates Papias as a " hearer of John and companion of Polycarp," he qualifies his words by saying, " But Papias has by no means represented him in the preface of his book as one who himself heard and saw the holy apostles: he teaches, on the contrary, that he had received the matters of faith (τὰ τῆς πίστεως) from those who had had personal acquaintance with

them (παρὰ τῶν ἐκείνοις γνωρίμων). In like manner, he says, a little farther on in the same
chapter (iii. 39 : 4), Papias insists that he received the words of the apostles from their own
followers, and says that he himself drew from
the lips[147] of Aristion and the presbyter John ;
adding this, that Papias often mentions these
by name when giving in his book the communications which they made. It is not only incredible that Eusebius erred in this, it was, indeed, scarcely possible for him to do so. For,
as he had the whole work of Papias before him,
and was making selections for his own purposes, it could scarcely escape him, if Papias,
in one case or another, appealed to the direct
communication of an apostle, clear as it was to
him that he had known Aristion and the presbyter John.   And how wholly differently would
he have brought forward in his preface his
vouchers, had they been the apostles ! he surely
would not have written, as he has, words which
are capable of a double interpretation, if he had
been referring directly to them.   In the whole
passage, however, the presbyters are set in con-

trast with the apostles; and yet the clause,
" the disciples of the Lord," subjoined to the
names Aristion and John the presbyter, makes
the meaning of this expression obscure; at
least rendering a double interpretation of it
possible. And is it credible that Papias should
say that he would confirm with his own declara-
tions the statement of the apostles? Respecting the words of the presbyters, he could say
this with the more justice, because, as his own
words and the declaration of Eusebius show,
he was able to use of these only Aristion and
John; but in the case of the others, he had to
rely on what was communicated indirectly.
Irenæus brings evidence confirmatory of this
way of interpreting the term " presbyters; "
for he derives the tradition of the " wanton
luxury of the kingdom of a thousand years "
expressly from the mouth of " the presbyters
who had seen John, the disciple of the Lord,"
and confirms this by appealing directly to the
writings of Papias. Granting in this way that
he was a hearer of John and a friend of Polycarp, it is perfectly clear that the presbyters in

Irenæus have the same signification as in Papias, and that they are not for an instant to be confounded with the apostles.¹⁴⁸ This inference respecting Papias which is found in Irenæus rests in the greatest probability on no other ground than the statement of Papias himself, carefully drawn up by Eusebius, but carelessly used by Irenæus; but that he confounded the apostle John, as his manner of speaking would indicate, is consistent with the fact that, as can be shown, the personality of the presbyter John, who likewise lived and died at Ephesus, was forgotten at a very early day.¹⁴⁹ We ought not to overlook the chronological difficulty connected with the supposition that Papias, who, according to the oldest testimony, suffered martyrdom about the same time as Polycarp, i. e. 165, was not able to collect the materials for his work among surviving apostles (παρὰ τῶν πρεσβυτέρων). How little the contents, so far as we know them, correspond to what we should expect from a work written by a disciple of the apostles, who is recording what he learned from their own lips, may be judged from what we will proceed to give.

Eusebius cites explicitly from the contents of that work of Papias, that the daughters of Philip informed him at Hierapolis of the resurrection of a dead man immediately subsequently to their father's time, and that Justus Barsabbas had drunken a goblet of poison without experiencing any injury. (Both of these accounts might be brought into relation with expressions of our Lord, as in fulfillment of them.) In addition, Papias asserted (we give the accounts in Eusebius iii. 39 : 5 literally) that he had learned many things through oral tradition, as well as some unknown (ξένας, strange) parables and teachings of the Lord, and other things, which were all too fabulous " (μνθικώτερα). To this class Eusebius assigns the doctrine of a kingdom of a thousand years' duration, which was to appear sensible on the earth after the resurrection of the dead. The representation of this kingdom was not given by Eusebius, but by Irenæus It runs as follows : " Then shall come the days in which vinestocks shall appear,

12

each one putting forth ten thousand branches, each branch ten thousand shoots, each shoot ten thousand clusters of grapes, and each cluster twenty-five measures of wine; and if one of the saints should try to take hold of one of the clusters, another of the latter will cry, I am better; lay hold of me, and praise the Lord by me. In like manner, an ear of corn will bring forth ten thousand ears, and each ear ten thousand grains," etc. This representation is made by Papias, as Irenæus testifies, to refer to the "elders," and, through them, even to John. Eusebius remarks, in reference to it, that Papias, a man of very inconsiderable mental parts, as his whole book shows, gathered his notions from misapprehended expressions of the apostles. He then goes oñ to say that there are other sayings of the Lord, dating from Aristion and John the presbyter, recorded in the book of Papias; but he refers those who may be interested in them to the work itself. To this he adds that he will subjoin to what has been already cited what he has learned respecting Mark. This runs, " And this says the presby

ter : " Mark, the interpreter of Peter, wrote carefully down all that he recollected, but not according to (τάξει) the order of Christ's speaking or working; for he neither heard Christ,
nor was a direct follower of him, but of Peter,
as already intimated, who always held his discourses as circumstances made it expedient,
but do not seek to arrange the sayings of the
Lord in any regular order. Mark accomplished
all that he purposed in writing what he had to
record just as he remembered it. There was
one thing, however, which he did keep in mind;
that was, not to omit anything that he had
heard, or to falsify anything which he undertook to set down." To this statement of Papias, which, judging by its tone, possibly only
refers in its first part to the presbyter, Eusebius subjoins a second statement respecting
Matthew, as follows: " This is what Papias
records respecting Mark; but of Matthew he
says, ' Matthew recorded in the Hebrew language the sayings of the Lord, but he translated every one of them as best he could." In
these words much is obscure : especially doubt-

ful is it whether we have rightfully translated
" sayings of the Lord ; " [150] at least the casual
words of Mark, " what Christ spoke and did,"
would seem to make it probable that both acts
and words were comprehended under the single
word " sayings." But do these expressions of
the presbyter and of Papias — and this is the
main question — relate to the two Gospels in
our possession bearing the names of Matthew
and Mark ? And if the expression, " sayings
of the Lord," is to remain unmolested, it does
not follow that a historical clothing of these
sayings is to be excluded, since neither Eusebius nor any other theologian of Christian antiquity supposed that the words of Papias stood
in antagonism with the two Gospels. If in our
time the inference has been drawn from the
words of Papias, that our Gospel according to
Mark is to be regarded only in a secondary
sense as the work of Mark, and is to be regarded as a subsequent revision of a work once
written by Mark, but which was lost sight of
at a very early date, the idea would show itself
to be a manifest freak of fancy. It would have

no other mission than to open to the freest play
of conjecture all our investigations respecting
the origin and the mutual relations of our three
synoptical Gospels.

True as this is of Mark, it is no less true of
Matthew. The statement of Papias has its
point in this, that it ascribes only a Hebrew
text to Matthew even. If this statement have
a satisfactory basis, even if we accept the other,
viz., that every one translated it as well as he
could, it leaves a broad margin between the
primitive Hebrew and our Greek Matthew.
That Hebrew text, like the primitive Mark,
must have been lost at a very early date, as not
a single one of the church Fathers saw or used
it. This gives rise to one of the most intricate
of questions, the discussion of which, however,
would not be in place here. We, on our side,
are fully satisfied in the matter, being convinced
that the acceptance by Papias of a primitive Hebrew text of Matthew (a view which may not
have been limited to him, and may have been
repeated by others) rested entirely upon a misunderstanding. I will briefly indicate of what

character it was, and whence it arose. The Judo-Christian struggles which sprung into being during the lifetime of the apostle Paul come more and more markedly into the foreground. There were two parties specially prominent : that of the Nazaræans was more moderate than the one more closely allied to philosophical speculation, the Ebionites. Both made use of a Gospel which bore the name of Matthew, the former in the Hebrew language, the latter in the Greek, the same document to which reference was made on a preceding page as the Gospel of the Hebrews. That they did. not hesitate to make modifications according to their own taste, in the text as they originally received it, is clear from the standpoint which they occupied, that of being the only sect characterized by strong self-will. And what we have really learned of this Gospel shows, as already stated, not only the great similarity to our Matthew, but also arbitrary deviations which have been made from him in some instances. When it was said later — I mean in the course of the second century — that the Nazaræans, a race dating from the very emergence of Christianity, possessed Matthew in the Hebrew, what was more natural than for one and another to assume, wholly in accordance with the claims of the Judo-Christian heretics, that Matthew himself wrote in Hebrew, and that the Greek text, the one which was circulated not only in the church, but among other Judo-Christians, was a translation? No one knew, no one made inquiries how divergent the two versions were; and not only were such investigations foreign to the character of the times, but the exclusiveness of the Nazaræans especially drew them away from such researches, making their home, as they did, apart, in the neighborhood of the Dead Sea.

Jerome gives us the benefit of his support in this explanation of the statement of Papias. Jerome, who was especially skilled in Hebrew, gained the temporary use of a Hebrew Gospel of the Nazaræans, and at once proclaimed that that was the primitive text of Matthew. Going deeper into the matter, however, he simply said that many held this Hebrew text to be the

original from Matthew's own hand; he translated it, moreover, into Greek and Latin, and
made some comments upon it. From these, as
well as from some fragments preserved by the
Fathers of the church, it may be shown that the
view represented by many scholars of late, and
in a certain sense shared with Papias, that the
so-called Hebrew Gospel is older than Matthew,
must be received in its very opposite form;
that that Hebrew book is a perversion of our
Greek Matthew, whose record bears the marks
in the whole of its diction, and especially in the
form of its Old Testament quotations, of being
no translation, but an original. That same independence of our Matthew is to be marked in
the Greek version of the Hebrew Gospel current among the Ebionites, only with this dis-
tinction, that here the heretical character may,
in consequence of the various hands which executed it, have assumed a more decided character.
Being in Greek, it was better known in the
church than the Hebrew version; and in the very
earliest epoch it was held to be another text of
Matthew. This agrees with what Papias wrote

respecting the various versions of Matthew,
among which he reckoned the Greek Matthew
then held by the church.

There is still more to be said of Papias and
his work. In relation to his efforts to obtain
materials he wrote that he believed that less
was needed in consequence of what was already
written in books. To what books did he refer?
May it not have been our own Gospels? The
expression used would make this not impossible, but the whole character of the book would
render it in the highest degree improbable ; for
he made no secret of his object of preparing, on
the ground of what was then, about A. D. 130 or
140,[151] related regarding the Saviour, a kind of
supplement to the Gospels, and he may or may
not have directed special reference to the prophetical allusions to the Lord. The Gospels,
therefore, he could not have used as sources,
and as affording materials for his collections.
The books referred to by him must be understood as rather relating to unauthentic and
more or less apocryphal records of the Lord's
career, of which there were so many from the

earliest date. These he set over against the
oral communications which he had received,
whose authenticity, as it could be traced
through the elders back to the apostles themselves, like the evangelical writings, seemed to
be unquestionable.

From that part of Papias's work which Eusebius thought was worth preserving, I have already cited the story of the resurrection from
the dead which the daughters of Philip asserted
that they had heard of their father, and also
the account of Justus Barsabbas and the poison.
In a third passage, where the Gospel of the
Hebrews gives its corroborative evidence, he repeats the story of a woman who had been accused before Jesus of sin. In like manner it
was stated in his book, as we learn of Catenen
and Œkumenius, that Judas the betrayer was
of such monstrous corpulence that he was
crushed by a carriage in a narrow street, and
that his bowels gushed out in consequence.
Regarding the further contents of the book,
Eusebius informs us, as already remarked,
that, in addition to a few matters altogether

fabulous, it contained a few parables and sayings of our Lord, hitherto unknown but utterly
unworthy of being recorded; and no ecclesiastical writer has done so, excepting in the case of
Irenæus's strange account of the kingdom which
should last a thousand years. In addition to
this, Anastasius Sinaita has called attention to
the fact that Papias has made the days of creation and paradise refer to Christ and the
church; and Andrew the Cappadocian, in his
Commentary on the Apocalypse, quoted a remark of Papias respecting the angels who had
been unfaithful to their trust in the government of the world. The latter writer, as does
Arethas also, cites the authority of Papias in
support of the credibility (Arethas uses the word
" inspiration ") of the Apocalypse.[152]

In view of all that has been said above, is
Papias's book one which can be accepted as
throwing important light upon the history of
our Gospels? The judgment of Eusebius respecting the man, that he was of limited understanding, is justified not only by the details
which are brought into view, but confirmed by

the fact that his alleged contributions to our
evangelical literature have been utterly disre-
garded by the church. What would not a single parable of the Lord be worth if its authenticity could be substantiated! But no one has
taken the slightest notice of all that has been
recorded by Papias; the fabulous character
which Eusebius charges upon the book — a man
himself characterized by extreme critical acumen — has adhered to the whole work, and it is
very unfair to trace this charge to a preposses-
sion in favor of the Chiliasts. The question
which has been raised we must answer in the
negative, in view not only of the character of
the man but also of the tendency of his book,
although the passage referring to Matthew and
Mark shows that that sort of matter was not
absolutely excluded.   However much to be
wished, however important it is to see light
thrown upon that very early Christian literature of which we find indications in the preface
to Luke, in order to enable us to see the origin
and the mutual relation of our synoptic Gospels cleared up, yet there is no use to be made

of Papias's statements so far as they stand alone
and in contradiction to the sufficiently authenticated facts of his time. If he has nevertheless
become a torch-bearer of critical theology in
our time, and a leader under whose guidance
we can be content to see the first two Gospels
divided up into what are called their authentic
and unauthentic constituent parts, there is little
result gained thereby other than the rearing of
an undeserved memorial to the bishop of Hierapolis.

Papias is the most acceptable and important
ally of the opponents of John's Gospel. And
why? Papias is silent respecting this Gospel.
Strauss and Renan, with their followers,[153] make
great account of this silence as opposed to the
belief in the authenticity of John's Gospel, and
evidently consider it something which can not
be surmounted. I fear that my readers would
not find it so after what has been said above
respecting the value of Papias's book. Does it
not betray — I ask the reader himself — complete ignorance of what Papias has said regarding his own undertaking, to quote him as

evidence against the Gospel of John? His remarks respecting Mark and Matthew make no difference in the character of his whole book. It is insisted, however, that Papias can not, from his silence, have known anything about the Gospel of John, still less have acknowledged its authenticity. Naturally here was supposed to be nothing less than decisive evidence against the genuineness of this Gospel; yet Papias, the bishop of Hierapolis, belonged even to the neighborhood of Ephesus, whence John's Gospel must have gone forth into the world, and his work can scarcely have been written prior to the middle of the second century. A more groundless and trivial demand can hardly be made than to grant that the silence of Papias respecting the Gospel of John constitutes a strong argument against its genuineness. For, in the first place, to give evidence respecting this Gospel formed no part whatever of the plan of Papias; and in the second place, from the fact that Eusebius has cited nothing from Papias's book respecting it, no inference can justly be drawn that there was noth-

ing in that book which related to John's
Gospel. The remarks respecting Mark and
Matthew are not cited by Eusebius in confirmation of the genuineness of their Gospels, but
simply in consequence of certain facts which
they touch upon. In the case of John — and
this is the only inference which can be ration-
ally drawn from the silence of Eusebius —
there were no circumstances which made it
necessary to cite what related to him.

Since, however, the opponents of John's Gospel have made so much account of the silence
of Eusebius in this matter, I can not refrain
from laying before the reader the great error into
which they have fallen. They completely overlook the purpose which Eusebius had in view
in writing. Respecting his object he expresses
himself plainly enough (iii. 3 : 2), where he says
that he wanted to trace in the ecclesiastical
writers what portion of the Antilegomena of
the New Testament they had made use of, and
what they have said about the Homologoumena,
as well as what does not fall under this head.[154]
Every one can see that this does not mean that

he meant to inquire which writings, both of the
Antilegomena as well as the Homologoumena,
they had used. In the case of the Antilegomena, or New Testament writings of doubtful
authority, the object is to indicate the use of
passages cited, and in this way to make clear
that this or that document was recognized. A
similar effort is not made by him in the case
of the Homologoumena, or writings invariably
recognized as authentic, but he seeks as ear-
nestly as in the case of the other class, to collect
ancient references to them, and what was an-
ciently known respecting them. That this construction of his purpose is the only correct one,
Eusebius shows not only in the case of Papias,
but of all other writers who happen to come
under his notice. He never says respecting
any one of the Gospels, This one or that one has
made use of it: this is much oftener the case
in the allusion to the Catholic Epistles,[155] than
to the Hebrews and the Apocalypse. But when
he cites what he finds in the older writers relative to the Gospels, he brings forward all that
refers to their origin, the time when they were

written, and the occasion which gave them
birth. This is the case with Irenæus, of whom
Eusebius writes (v. 8) the following: "Matthew wrote his Gospel among the Hebrews, in
their own language, while Peter and Paul were
preaching in Rome and strengthening the
church. After their death, Mark, the disciple
and interpreter of Peter, wrote, recording what
Peter had preached. Luke, the companion of
Paul, took down the Gospel as it was announced
by the latter, and subsequently John, the disciple who lay on the Lord's breast, wrote his
Gospel during his sojourn at Ephesus." Very
instructive, moreover, are the extracts from
Clement. Eusebius says (vi. 14) that Clement
briefly treats in his Hypotyposa all the biblical
writings, not passing over the Antilegomena.
"I mean," he goes on to say literally, "the
Epistle of Jude, the other Catholic Epistles, that
of Barnabas, and the Revelation ascribed to
Peter." He allows the Epistle to the Hebrews
to have been written by Paul, but in the Hebrew
language. After further remarks respecting
this Epistle, Eusebius goes on to say: "But in
13

the same treatise Clement communicates a tradition of the following import respecting the
true order of the Gospels; those were first
written which contain a genealogical record.
Mark's Gospel, moreover, had the following origin: When Peter was publicly preaching in
Rome, and, filled with the Spirit, was announ-
cing the Gospel, Mark was urged by many who
were present, to put on record the statements
of Peter, since he had long been Peter's companion and could remember the substance of
his discourses; and when in accordance with
this request he wrote his Gospel, he communicated it to those who had asked for it. Peter,
on his part, when he learned what Mark was
doing, neither took ground against it, nor urged
him to continue in it. And John, when he saw
that that physical, active side of the Saviour
had been fully delineated in the first three
Gospels, gratified the wish of friends that he
should portray Jesus on the spiritual side.
This is what Clemens communicates." We
add to this what Eusebius (vi. 35) has taken, of
similar purport, from Origen: that from tradi-

tion he had gathered that one of the four Gospels which had universal credence in God's
church on earth, the one bearing the name of
Matthew, at first a collector of customs and
then an apostle of Jesus, was the one first written; and that it was composed in the Hebrew
tongue and dedicated to believers who had
come out from Judaism. The second in the
order of the writing was Mark's, who had followed Peter's lead, and whom Peter himself
recognizes in his catholic epistle as his son, —
"My son Mark greeteth you." The third was
Luke's, defended by Paul, and prepared for the
use of those who were converted from heathen-
dom. All these were followed by the one which
bears the name of John.

Now does not a glance show that all these
passages from Irenæus, Clemens and Origen
were not quoted by Eusebius for the purpose of
proving the genuineness of the Gospels, and
just as little what Papias has to say about Mark
and Matthew, but that they were recorded
merely as interesting facts relative to the dis-

tinctive history of each one of the evangelical
records ?

But we have the most striking confirmation
of our view in extracts from writers still older,
whose clear and distinct testimony to our Gospels and other Homologoumena, such as the
Pauline Epistles, are passed over by Eusebius
in accordance with his general design, while he
records what seemed to him to support the
Antilegomena.   Here Papias himself is at the
head ; at any rate Eusebius remarks expressly
respecting him at the end of his treatise, that
he had used proof texts from the First Epistle
of John, and also from that of Peter.[156]   Further
he says (iv. 18: 3) of Justin, that he had borne
in mind the Apocalypse of John, and expressly
allowed that it was written by the apostle ;
but of the quotations from the Gospels found
in him, he does not have a syllable.   From
Polycarp's Epistle to the Philippians he draws
the statement (iv. 14) that he was indebted
for many proof texts to the First Epistle of Peter ; but of the far more numerous Pauline
citations, taken from the majority of Paul's

Epistles, he says nothing.[157] Of Clemens Romanus he remarks that he had taken many
ideas from the Epistle to the Hebrews, and often
in the original words, while he passes in silence
over all quotations from the Pauline Epistles.
From the three books of Theophilus to Autolycus, and from the one directed against the
heresy of Hermogenes, he cites (iv. 14) nothing
further than that in the latter he makes use of
passages in the Apocalypse of John; and yet
Theophilus often and unmistakably uses the
Pauline Epistles (e. g. Rom. ii. 6, et seq. ad Autolyc. i. 14; Rom. xiii. 7, et sq. ad Autolyc. iii.
14); he even (and this is the most pertinent to
our needs) cites the Gospel of John under that
very appellation.

With all this, do we not apprehend the aim
of what Eusebius records?   And may we not
steer clear of the long-continued perversion[158] of
his purpose?   On our part, we are of the firm
conviction that it needs only an upright determination to discern the truth as it is in order
to see the complete worthlessness of this famous
Papias argument against the Gospel of John.

The absurdity of the argument that the unfortunate Bishop of Hierapolis, shortly before
the middle of the second century, knew nothing of the writings of Luke and the Epistles of
Paul, because, judging by Eusebius's silence,
he made no mention of them, has been long
perceived; but very recently it has been set
aside[159] by those who are the rudest opponents
of ecclesiasticism, on the ground that the bishop
may have been silent about things which he
knew, but which seemed too trivial to mention. Still less trouble has it caused this party
that, according to Eusebius's express testimony,
Papias made use of the First Epistle of John.
In the place, some pages back, where we had
occasion to refer to Polycarp's use of this same
Epistle, it was said that the evidence in favor
of this Epistle is equally applicable to the Gospels; but we asserted that not only had the
identity of authorship in these two treatises
been called into question, but that there has been
a hasty impulse to cast the Epistle itself overboard. Thus Papias's silence was to bring the
Gospel into utter disrepute, while, with his dis-

tinct testimony, he could not shield the Epistle from the attacks of overbearing critics.

In view of such proceedings, it is a genuine satisfaction to know that there has recently been brought to light a work printed long ago, but quite forgotten, in which Papias and his book give direct testimony in behalf of the Gospel, which is assaulted under the protection of his name. It is a prologue to the Gospel of John in a Latin manuscript of the Vatican (leaf 244), which, by a note in an old hand, is traced back to the possession of the Bohemian, Duke Wenceslaus (iste liber creditur fuisse Divi Venceslai Ducis Boemiæ), and which, according to the appearances of the writing, dates from the ninth century. It is now designated Vat. Alex. No. 14.[160] The prologue discloses that it was composed prior to the time of Jerome, and begins with the words, " Evangelium iohannis manifestatum et datum est ecclesiis ab iohanne adhuc in corpore constituto, sicut papias nomine hierapolitanus discipulus iohannis carus in exotericis id est in extremis quinque libris retulit." There can be no stronger testimony than this that Papias did give evidence in behalf of John's Gospel. The further purport of the prologue is, with all its brevity, rich in surprising facts. That it sprang from the work of Papias seems, however, on more grounds than one, to be doubtful; and on this account the credibility of the other matters which it communicates can not be put on the same footing with the first.[161]

Before leaving Papias, however, we must revert to one source of evidence in favor of John's Gospel, which Irenæus (v. 36 : 2) cites even from the lips of the presbyters, those high authorities of Papias : " And on this account they say that the Lord used the expression, ' In my Father's house are many mansions' " (John xiv. 2). As the presbyters put this expression[162] in connection with the degrees of elevation granted to the just in the City of God, in Paradise, in Heaven, according as they bring their thirty, sixty, or a hundred-fold from the harvest, so nothing is more probable than that Irenæus borrowed this whole expression of the presbyter, together with the portraiture already referred to of the kingdom of a thousand years, from the work of Papias. Whether it comes from that source, however, or not, on every ground the authority of the presbyters stands higher than that of Papias; it takes us back unquestionably to the close of the apostolical period. In what way, and with what machinery, the noted men with whom unbelief becomes an art, and whose very efforts to propagate it are labored at with artistic ingenuity, will be able to set aside this evidence in support of John's Gospel, and, together with the testimony of the presbyters, that of Papias in the Latin prologue to John, is not apparent to me; yet I do not doubt that the skill which has defied all efforts to baffle it as yet, will be able to meet and overcome even this obstacle.

And lastly, we have to trace the bearings of New Testament textual criticism on the question under discussion. This is the science which has to do with the primitive documents of the sacred text, the direct bearer of saving truth. Investigation into these primitive documents ought to throw light upon the history of

the sacred text; i. e. we ought to learn from
them what in all times Christendom has united
in finding recorded in the books which contain
the New Testament; this, e. g., what Colum-
ba, the pious and learned Irish monk of the
sixth century; what Ambrose at Milan, and
Augustine in Africa, in the fourth century;
what Cyprian and Tertullian, in the third and
second centuries, found recorded in their Latin
copies of the New Testament: in like manner,
what Photius, the patriarch of Constantinople,
in the tenth; Cyril, the Bishop of Jerusalem, in
the fifth; Athanasius and Origen of Alexandria,
in the fourth and third centuries, found on record in the Greek copies of their time.   The
final and highest object of these investigations
consists in this, however,— to trace with exact-
ness those expressions and words which the
holy apostles either wrote with their own hand
or dictated to others.   If the New Testament
is the most important and most hallowed book
in the world, we must certainly lay the greatest value on all efforts to possess the text in
which it was originally written in its most per-

fect state, without omissions, without additions, and without changes. Should it be impossible to attain this result, still the task would at any rate be ours to approximate as closely as possible to the primitive form of the text.

The question will at once recur to many readers, Do our ordinary editions of the Bible not contain the genuine and true text? The German Protestant, with his Luther's Bible in his hand, would ask this question ; so would the Catholic, with his Latin Vulgate, or his German or French translation of it; so would the Englishman, with his Authorized Version; so too would the Russian, with his Sclavonic text. The answer to this question, viewed from what side we will, is not light. Every one of these translations has again its own more or less rich text-history, and there is no one which has not enough of the original to insure the degree of faith necessary to salvation. But if the effort be made to see how closely each follows the original, how truly each has preserved the text as it was given by the apostles, it must be compared with the original text, from which, directly or indirectly, all have flowed. We know that the Greek is the original text of the New Testament. And how is it with the genuineness of this text?

When the discovery of printing, in the first quarter of the sixteenth century, was applied to the publication of the Greek New Testament, Erasmus, at Bâle, and Cardinal Ximenes, at Alcala, took as the basis of the work such manuscripts as were at their command. Their editions were repeated elsewhere, often with slight modification of the original text, according to other manuscripts. The learned Parisian printer, Robert Stephens, introduced some such modifications; the Elzevir followed, the work of a Leyden printer; and soon the force of usage became so powerful that the theologians accepted the text as it was established by the Erasmus, Elzevir, and Robert Etienne editions as a kind of authorized general edition. In the mean time, scholars had begun to trace new sources, — Greek manuscripts written in the first century, as well as manuscripts prepared for the translations effected in the first five cen-

turies into Latin, Gothic, Coptic, Ethiopian,
Armenian ; to these may be added the textual
readings which are found recorded in the works
of the church Fathers of the second century.
From this there issued at last the result that,
under the hand of the various transcribers,
learned as well as unlearned, the New Testament text has assumed extraordinary diversity
in its readings. And, although this diversity
is, in thousands of passages, limited to merely
grammatical forms, having no relation to the
sense, there is no lack of places which involve
more important matters, and which are of historical and dogmatic value. After this had
gone on so far that the whole of Christendom
was interested in the highest degree in the
matter, earnest men, with whom it was a sacred
duty to ascertain what is truth rather than to
conform with established usage, conceived that
it was their especial task to reform the ordinary text by incorporating upon it the results
of examining the ancient but later discovered
manuscripts. Still, it is only in the most recent
period that men have dared to lay aside the

ordinary text, which had no scientific guaranty of authenticity, and to bring into exclusive use the text of the earliest documents. For it needs no proof that the oldest documents, those which run back to within a few centuries of the first composition, must be truer to the original than those which were written a thousand years or more subsequently to the first composition. In giving the preference to the most ancient documents, however, there is the rigid duty of examining them most carefully in respect to their intrinsic character and their mutual relations. With this is to be coupled the fact that our various most ancient manuscripts give the text with a great diversity of readings, through which cause their use is made much more difficult in establishing the original text given by the apostles. All the more necessary was it, therefore, to seek the oldest and most trustworthy of them all. In order to do this, Richard Bentley considered it important to give the preference to that text which shows the closest accordance with the oldest Greek documents and the Latin text of the fourth century. In

accordance with Bentley's judgment, Carl Lach-
mann undertook, with very few aids, the restoration of the text which was generally diffused
in the fourth century ; for there seems to be no
possibility of reaching any documentary evidence which goes back of that age. There is
no doubt that the earliest Latin translation of
the Gospels — to limit ourselves to this — was
written soon after the middle of the second
century ; for, as I have had occasion to remark
above, the Latin translator of Irenæus, before
the close of the second century, and Tertullian
in the last decade of the same century, appear
to have been in undisputed dependence upon
it. This oldest translation we possess [163] at the
present time, — certainly in its main body ; for
our oldest documents, reaching back to the fifth
century, and which bear relation to the text
which was prepared in North Africa, the home
of Tertullian, find a frequent confirmation of
their readings in the two witnesses already
mentioned, the translators of Irenæus and Tertullian. And on this account, in behalf of
those texts which men have not recorded in

their writings, it must be admitted that they correspond to the very earliest edition, or are very nearly allied to it. By the discovery of the Sinaitic manuscript we have advanced yet farther ; for this text, which, on palæographical grounds, has been assigned by competent schol- ars to the middle of the fourth century, stands in such surprising alliance with the oldest Latin translation that it is really to be regarded as coincident with the text which, soon after the middle of the second century, served the first Latin translator, the preserver of the so-called Itala, as a foundation.   And that this text was not an isolated one is manifest from the fact that the oldest Syrian text, contained in a man- uscript of the fifth century, lately discovered in the Nitrian desert, as well as Origen and others of the earliest Fathers, stands in specially close connection with it.   The Syrian text just men- tioned possesses on its side a power of carrying conviction quite analogous to the Itala, and manifesting it in that double way which I have endeavored to set forth ; for the latest investi- gations leave no doubt that the Peshito, which

is universally ascribed to the close of the second
century, presupposes the existence of the Nitrian text, so that the latter must have arisen
about the middle of the second century.

What now follows from all these considerations in the way of answering the question
which has been raised? Two things we have
to make use of and apply in the most emphatic
manner. At the very outset of this work I
have indicated it as a noteworthy fact, that soon
after the middle, and even about the middle, of
the second century, the four Gospels underwent
an undoubted common translation, and appeared in a Latin as well as in a Syriac version.
These translations not only prove the same
thing which the harmonistic treatment of the
Gospels by Tatian of Syria and by Theophilus
at almost the same epoch proves; they prove at
the same time much more, namely, that as the
Gospels of Luke and John were in existence at
that time in the same form in which we have
them now, so were those of Matthew and Mark.
If isolated citations from the oldest epoch allow
the suspicion that instead of our Matthew, the

14

nearly related and only subsequently discriminated Gospel of the Hebrews was perhaps
used, or that even our Mark had then taken
that primitive form which is indicated in the
recent investigations of Papias's account, yet
the oldest Latin texts of these Gospels completely exclude this suspicion, at least so far as
the middle of the second century is concerned.
They give thoughtful investigators as little
ground for believing that these texts might
shortly before have been developed by unknown
hands from a previous form, and now in an
unskillful fashion, after the change which has
been wrought upon them by the Latin Church,
are held to be the original draft. Even here
the Nitrian text stands by the side of the
Itala in confirmation of it, omitting, however,
the Gospel of Mark, with the exception of
the last four verses. It is well known that
the discoverer and editor of this text uttered his conviction, and strengthened it with
plausible proofs, that in the case of the Gospel
of Matthew this text may have sprung from
the original Hebrew form. In opposition to

this decidedly erroneous impression, the agreement of the same Syrian text with our oldest
Greek and Latin documents confirms in the
most striking manner our conclusion in relation to the Greek text of Matthew, as well as
the conclusion that in the middle of the second
century there was no other text of Matthew
than the one which we possess. And so far as
Mark is concerned, this Syrian translator bears
witness in support of the closing verses already
employed by Irenæus, which, according to decisive critical authority, are not genuine, but
which were appended to the accepted text of
Mark's Gospel.[164]

But I have yet another matter of textual
criticism to take note of, which in my judgment affords evidence that our collective Gospels are to be traced back at least to the beginning of the second or the end of the first century. As on the one side the text of the Sinaitic manuscript, together with the oldest Itala
text, is to be assigned specifically to the use of
the second century, so on the other side it is easy
to establish that that same text, in spite of all

its superiority over other documents, had assumed even their differences in many respects
from the primitive purity of the reading, and
that it even then presupposed a complete text-
history.   We are not directed in this exclusively to the Codex Sinaiticus and one or another
of the Itala manuscripts, together with Irenæus
and Tertullian : but we can accept all these
documents, which we must assign, partly from
necessity and partly with the greatest probability, to the second century ; the fact is undeniable that there was even then a rich text-history.   We mean by this that even prior to the
second half of the second century, while copy
after copy of our Gospels was made, not only
are there many errors of transcribers to be
found, but the phraseology and the sense in
particular places are changed, and larger or
smaller additions are made from apocryphal
and oral sources.   With all this, such changes
are not excluded which were the result of putting together separate parallel passages, and
these testify in a striking manner to the early
union of our Gospels in a single canon.   If this

is really the case, there is an important stadium of the textual history of our four Gospels prior to the middle of the second century, prior to the time when canonical authority, together with the more settled ecclesiastical order, made arbitrary changes in the sacred text more and more difficult, — this I shall take occasion to show fully at another time, — and for the lapse of this history we must assume at least a half century. According to this, must not — I dare not say the origin of the Gospels, but — the establishment of the evangelical canon be set at the close of the first century? And is not this result all the more certain from the coincidence with it of all the historical factors of the second century, which we have reviewed without any reserve?

There will be those, it is not to be doubted, who will accuse us of one-sidedness and want of thoroughness. And in truth we have passed over some things whose examination would have been in accordance with my purpose to pass in review all the oldest documents which could throw light upon the Gospels or illumi-

nate their primitive recognition. If we have
omitted anything, it is only because the inferences to be drawn from them touch too closely,
as it has seemed to us,—perhaps wrongly,—
upon the domain of hypothesis to give really
solid results to our investigation. But in what
we have passed over there is nothing which is
antagonistic to what has been already advanced.
We allude, e. g., to the earliest traces of a ca-
nonic indication and collection of apostolic writings, including the earliest appendices to the
New Testament, and contained in a portion of
the New Testament itself as the church established it in the fourth century. This is certainly
the most recent portion, viz., the Second Epistle
of Peter, where, (iii. 16), reference is made
not only to the collection of the Pauline Epistles, but of other New Testament writings ; [165]
also the closing verses of John's Gospel, of
which verse twenty-fourth is held with the most
correctness as the oldest testimony from the
hand of a presbyter of Ephesus in favor of
John's authorship.[166] The Testaments of the
twelve patriarchs,[167] too, contain undeniable

traces of an acquaintance with the books of the
New Testament, the Gospels as well as the
Pauline Epistles and the Apocalypse; they confirm, therefore, the existence of a collection of
the books of the New Testament at the time
when they were written, and this time can
scarcely be set later than the close of the first
or the opening of the second century.[168] But
so far as definite details are concerned, such as
can be drawn into active service by those who
are most determined in their opposition to
John's Gospel, we can discover nothing but
misunderstanding and unjustified conclusions.
It is a misunderstanding, for example, to bring
the celebration in Asia Minor of the feast of
the Passover into antagonism with the Gospel
of John; for the festival as it is celebrated
there, which builds simply upon the example of
John, is erroneously understood as if it related
to the Last Supper, while it really commemo-
rates the death of Jesus the true paschal Lamb
(1 Cor. v. 7), the historic basis being given for
it in John's Gospel. But when men bring the
relation of John's to the synoptic Gospels as

the ground for suspicion respecting the apostolic origin of the former, and cite the pecu-
liarity of John's diction, as well as that of the
Apocalypse, the universal character of his Gospel compared with Gal. ii. 9, and its dogmatic
character, especially in relation to the person
of Christ, as brought into contrast with the history of the Christian doctrine, they profess to
know more than it is granted to man to
know, and use what is naturally hypothetical
and uncertain to throw doubts over what is
clear and fixed. Against tactics which rely
upon the appearance of knowledge and cun-
ningly shaped hypotheses, and which are
shrewdly devised to entrap the simple, there
is need of summoning the aid of definite and
ascertained facts.

We can only call it a welcome occurrence
that through the radical character of the two
most distinguished modern biographers of Jesus, the Tubingen fantasy-builder and the Parisian caricaturist, the contrasts between belief
and disbelief in the Gospels and the Lord
have been made thoroughly apparent. It is

only clear vision which leads to the gift of sure
decision. Never before have theologians joined
in with the Christian church and the whole
world of culture in demanding so appositely as
now, How is it down at the foundations, respecting our evangelical belief in the Lord? Nothing
is easier than to deceive those who are not in a
position which enables them to answer in a
scientific manner this greatest question of
Christendom ; nothing easier than to mislead
them under a pretense of learned and honest
investigation. Yet the character of this age
grants all license to thorough and honorable
inquiry in matters where, in former ages less
intelligent than ours, faith, and a faith too
that often enough was blind, had unquestioned
sway. It is just from this that many who have
not been able to enter deeply into this class of
studies have come to believe that if we look
at the matter thoroughly and scientifically
there is a great deal of doubt about the facts of
Jesus' life. And scarcely anything has had
more factitious influence in inducing this in-
credulity than the often-repeated statement that

the ancient history of the Christian church
gives the most conclusive testimony against the
genuineness of our Gospels, especially that of
John, in which the divine-human character of
the Saviour of the world stands forth to the
offense and confusion of an unchristian age
more manifestly than in the synoptic Gospels.
In the course of this investigation we have
been brought to exactly the opposite view. To
awaken doubts respecting the genuineness of
our Gospels, and John's especially, in the minds
of the lettered as well as the unlettered, to
cause many to deny them even, is the work of
that skeptical spirit which has attained to almost undisputed pre-eminence during the past
hundred years. And yet there are few instances
in the collective literature of antiquity of so
general and commanding assent being given to
works of a historical character as to our four
Gospels.

Against that kind of unbelief which has
taken root in the modern frivolous school of
religious literature, in that earth-born emanci-
pation of the human spirit which will allow of

no subjugation by the Spirit of God, science has no weapons. It is their unbelief which has incorporated itself into Renan's book : therein lies its power, its secret of success ; there is no need of learned inquiry respecting it : the parti-colored rags which it has borrowed of science only partially conceal the naked limbs. It is quite otherwise with the learned arguments which have been brought against the life of Jesus, and the historic attacks which have been made upon the authenticity of the evangelical sources. Here we have to protest with the utmost decisiveness, but on the ground of rigid scientific investigation. The victory of God in behalf of right belongs to truth alone. It is only a petty littleness of belief that can believe that the sacred interests of truth are imperiled by the use of those dishonored weapons which are so much in vogue in the present age. But whoever stands in the interest of that truth which is to enter into victory must display his faith in the result by no timid counting of costs, but by the constant exercise of his best knowledge and most conscientious endeavors.

NOTES

NOTE 1, p. 12.—Hilgenfeld's friends are more
outspoken in this matter than even he is, while
they. completely echo his words. Thus Volkmar,
p. 110 : " The Sinaitic Bible is asserted to have no
greater value or significance than to make certain
the fact that the canon of our four Gospels, as
well as the whole Old Catholic New Testament,
was in existence at the commencement of the
the second century." P. 120: " This which has
been added is, therefore, a ne plus ultra ; in this
phrase, scriptum est, are involved not only the
canonicity of Matthew, but the fourfoldness of
our Gospels, and the authenticity of the whole
New Testament." In like tone A. Ritschl, in the
Jahrb. für deutsch. Theol. 1866, 2d pt. p. 355 : " But
it is arbitrarily foisted upon the words of the here-
siarch, as it is also an arbitrary supposition, that
the church from the apostolic time down was furnished with the canon of the New Testament, and
with bishops who were the successors of the apostles. And whoever trusts Tertullian so far as the
former statement is concerned, has no right to re-

fuse to recognize with him the apostolical succes-
sion of bishops. As all the studies of Tischendorf.
into the history of the canon lead him to believe
that no one of the New Testament Scriptures can
be looked at by itself and as destitute of canonical
authority" [these words are intended to convey
the meaning that the canonization of Matthew, testified to by Barnabas, is to be confined to Matthew
alone. That they signify no less than that the beginning of a canon of the New Testament can not
be limited to a single document, can be clearly
seen in the passage cited, and is there fully dwelt
upon; the ascribing of another meaning is a perversion of my words], "and as he finds himself
obliged to assign the establishment of the canon to
the close of the first century . . . . If, now, it is
a result to be almost envied that one should convince himself so easily of the correctness of his
judgment respecting the history of the New Testament canon, they seem to be much more to be
envied who want to confirm this result by holding
firmly to the doctrine of an apostolical appoint-
ment of bishops who had authority commensurate
with that of the apostles." These last words are
a mere stupid joke, and are to be accounted as
such; they are, therefore, of the same character,
and are animated by the same spirit, as that which
has caused other men to heap calumny upon me.

NOTE 2, p. 14.—I might perhaps repel the charge

that an over-heated zealous activity, akin to that of the Spanish knight-errant, lies dormant in my words, by citing the expression of the " Wiener Allgem. Literatur Zeitung zunächst für das katholische Deutschland, No. 25: "So far as real learning and familiarity with the subject are concerned, Strauss compared with Tischendorf is a pigmy by a giant." . . . " One word of his weighs more than the whole book of another, however carefully prepared."

NOTE 3, p. 17. — Zur Quellenkritik des Epiphanios, 1865, p. 68 " Herakleon does not specifically mention Irenæus." P. 168 : "Epiphanios did not find the name of Herakleon mentioned in Irenæus, but he unquestionably learned of Hippolytus what he knew about him." "Even the order is given by Irenæus. And just because he does not mention Herakleon, Epiphanios thinks that he must put him behind Mark."

NOTE 4, p. 17. — This may do something toward clearing away the charge which has often been brought against me, that I have not read Justin and others, and merely copy what I find in " Introductions."

NOTE 5, p. 19.— The small, popular edition of this work has already been published in France by the Toulouse Société des livres religieux, in England

by the Religious Tract Society, and in America.
In the latter country a German edition has also
been issued. The French translator is Prof. Sard-
inoux of Montauban, the English translator Mr.
J. B. Heard, and the American, Prof. H. B. Smith.

NOTE 6, p. 25. — Tacit. Annal. xv. 44.

NOTE 7, p. 25. — Pliny's Epist. x. 97.

NOTE 8, p. 25. — The statement of Suetonius
(Claud. 25), that Claudius (about 52 after Christ)
banished the Jews from Rome because, incited by
Christ, they made a perpetual uproar, ought hardly
to be cited here.

NOTE 9, p. 28. — Renan, p. xxvii. On est tenté
de croire que Jean . . . fut froissé de voir qu'on
ne lui accordait pas dans l'histoire du Christ une
assez grande place ; qu'alors il commença à dicter
une foule de choses qu'il savait mieux que les autres,
avec l'intention de montrer que, dans beaucoup de
cas où on ne parlait que de Pierre, il avait figuré
avec et avant lui.

NOTE 10, p. 28. — Page xxvii. N'excluant pas
une certaine rivalité de l'auteur avec Pierre.

NOTE 11, p. 28. — Page xxvii. Sa haine contre
Judas, haine antérieure peut-être à la trahison.

NOTE 12, p. 28.—Page 403. Selon une tradition
Jésus aurait trouvé un appui dans la propre femme
du procurateur. Celle-ci avait pu entrevoir le
doux Galiléen de quelque fenêtre du palais, don-
nant sur les cours du temple. Peut-être le revit-
elle en songe, et le sang de ce beau jeune homme,
qui allait être versé, lui donna-t-il le cauchemar.

NOTE 13, p. 29.—Page 361. Peut-être Lazare,
pâle encore de sa maladie, se fit-il entourer de
bandelettes comme un mort et enfermer dans son
tombeau de famille. . . . L'émotion qu'éprouva Jésus près du tombeau de son ami, qu'il croyait mort,
put être prise par les assistants pour ce trouble, ce
frémissement qui accompagnaient les miracles;
l'opinion populaire voulant que la vertu divine fût
dans l'homme comme un principe épileptique et
convulsif. Jésus . . . désira voir encore une fois
celui qu'il avait aimé, et, la pierre ayant été écartée,
Lazare sortit avec ses bandelettes et la tête en-
tourée d'un suaire. . . Intimement persuadés que
Jésus était thaumaturge, Lazare et ses deux sœurs
purent aider un de ses miracles a s'exécuter . . .
L'état de leur conscience etait celui des stigma-
tisées, des convulsionnaires, des possédées de cou-
vent. . . . Quant à Jésus, il n'était pas plus maître
que Saint Bernard, que saint François d'Assise de
modérer l'avidité de la foule et de ses propres disciples pour le merveilleux. La mort, d'ailleurs,
allait dans quelques jours lui rendre sa liberté di-

15

vine, et l'arracher aux fatales nécessités d'un rôle
qui chaque jour devenait plus exigeant, plus diffi-
cile à soutenir.

NOTE 14, p. 29.—Matt. xxvi. 36, et sq.; Mark xiv.
32, et sq.; Luke xxii. 40, et sq.

NOTE 15, p. 30.—Page 378, et sq.

NOTE 16, p. 30.—Page 209.   La profonde
sécheresse de la nature aux environs de Jérusalem
devait ajouter au déplaisir de Jésus.

NOTE 17, p. 30.—Page 28.   Si jamais le monde
resté chrétien, mais arrivé à une notion meilleure
de ce qui constitue le respect des origines, veut
remplacer par d'authentiques lieux saints les sanc-
tuaires apocryphes et mesquins où s'attachait la pi-
été des âges grossiers, c'est sur cette hauteur de Nazareth qu'il bâtira son temple.   Là, au point d'ap-
parition du christianisme et . au centre d'action de
son fondateur, devrait s'élever la grande église où
tous les chrétiens pourraient prier.   Là aussi, sur
cette terre où dorment le charpentier Joseph et
des milliers de Nazaréens oubliés.

NOTE 18, p. 31.—Page 426.   Sa tête s'inclina
sur sa poitrine, et il expira.   Repose maintenant
dans ta gloire, noble initiateur.   Ton œuvre est
achevée ; ta divinité est fondée.   Ne crains plus de

voir crouler par une faute l'édifice de tes efforts.
Page 67. Toute l'historie du christianisme nais-
sant est devenue de la sorte une délicieuse pastor-
ale. Un Messie aux repas de noces, la courtisane et
le bon Zachée appelés à ses festins, les fondateurs
du royaume du ciel comme un cortége de para-
nymphes. Page 219. Le charmant docteur, qui
pardonnait à tous pourvu qu'on l'aimât, ne pouvait
trouver beaucoup d'écho dans ce sanctuaire des
vaines disputes et des sacrifices vieillis. Page 222.
L'orgueil du sang lui paraît l'ennemi capital qu'il
faut combattre. Jésus, en d'autres termes, n'est
plus juif. Il est révolutionnaire au plus haut de-
gré; il appelle tous les hommes â un culte fondé
sur leur seule qualité d'enfants de Dieu. Page 316.
Parfois on est tenté de croire que, voyant dans sa
propre mort un moyen de fonder son royaume, il
conçut de propos délibéré le dessein de se faire
tuer. D'autres fois la mort se présente à lui comme
un sacrifice, destiné à apaiser son Père et à sauver
les hommes. Un goût singulier de persécution et
de supplices le pénétrait. Son sang lui paraissait
comme l'eau d'un second baptême dont il devait
être baigné, et il semblait possédé d'une hâte
étrange d'aller au-devant de ce baptême qui seul
pouvait étancher sa soif.

Note 19, p. 36.—That this was the true date
when this catalogue was proposed, is rendered
more certain by the circumstance that the author

indicates the episcopate of Pius, which is generally computed to have extended from 142 to 157, by the words temporibus nostris and nuperrime, i. e. "in our time," and "very recently." And even when he follows his own conjectures, or those which were then general, respecting any matter, as, for example, his ascribing the "Shepherds," an apocalyptic book of edification, to Hermas the brother of Pius the Roman bishop, his chronological statements must still be conceded not to have lost any validity.

NOTE 20, p. 38. — See Iren. adv. hæres. iii. 11 : 8.

NOTE 21, p. 39. — See Iren. adv. hær. iii. 3: 4; and particularly his letter to Florinus in Euseb. Hist. Eccl. v. 20 (Iren. opp. ed. Stieren i. 822).

NOTE 22. p. 40. — In the Latin translation the passage runs: "Vidi enim te, quum adhuc puer (παῖς) essem, in inferiore Asia apud Polycarpum quum in imperatoria aula splendide ageres et illi (παρ᾽ αὐτῷ) te probare conareris. Nam ea quæ tunc gesta sunt melius memoria teneo, quam quæ nuper acciderunt (quippe quae pueri discimus, simul cum animo ipso coalescunt eique penitus inhærent) adeo ut et locum dicere possim in quo sedens beatus Polycarpus disserebat, processus quoque eius et ingressus vitæque modum et corporis speciem, sermones denique quos ad multitudinem

habebat; et familiarem consuetudinem quæ illi
cum Iohanne ac reliquis qui dominum viderant in-
tercessit, ut narrabat, et qualiter dicta eorum com-
memorabat: quæque de domino ex ipsis audiverat
de miraculis illius etiam ac de doctrina, quæ ab iis
qui verbum vitæ ipsi conspexerant acceperat Polycarpus, qualiter referebat, cuncta Scripturis con-
sona." The attempt to make these closing words
apply to the Old Testament, and not to the Gospels, is a most impotent attempt to take away all
point whatever from what Irenæus is saying.

NOTE 23, p. 43.—See adv. Marcion, iv. 2. Con-
stituimus inprimis evangelicum instrumentum apostolos auctores habere, quibus hoc munus evangelii promulgandi ab ipso domino sit compositum;
si et apostolicos, non tamen solos sed cum apostolis
et post apostolos. Denique nobis fidem ex apostolis Iohannes et Matthæus insinuant, ex apostol-
icis Lucas et Marcus instaurant.

NOTE 24, p. 43. — See adv. Marcion, iv. 5. In
summa si constat id verius quod prius, id prius
quod et ab initio, ab initio quod ab apostolis, pariter
utique constabit id esse ab apostolis traditum quod
apud ecclesias apostolorum fuerit sacrosanctum.

NOTE 25, p. 45. — See the document already referred to: Eadem auctoritas ecclesiarum ceteris
quoque patrocinabitur evangeliis, quæ proinde per

illas et secundum illas habemus, Johannis dico
[before this he says, habemus et Johanni alumnas
ecclesias] et Matthæi; licet et Marcus quod edidit
Petri affirmetur, cuius interpres Marcus. Nam
et Lucæ digestum Paulo adscribere solent; capit
magistrorum videri quæ discipuli promulgarint.

NOTE 26, p. 46. — Theophilus was appointed
bishop of Antioch, according to the statement of
Eusebius (Hist. Eccles. iv. 19 and 20), about the
eighth year of Marcus Aurelius's reign, i. e., about
168, at the same time that Soter was bishop of
Rome. The third book of his able Apology to
Autolycus he wrote, according to his own statement, in the year 181; the first two books in the
year 180. It is extremely probable that the compilation from the Gospels was intended to serve in
helping him discharge his official duties, — at the
outset, at least, of his term of service.

Tatian himself tells us (Orat. ad Græc. 19) that
when in Rome together with Justin he shared the
persecution experienced by the cynic philosopher
Crescens. After Justin had fallen as a martyr, Tatian left Rome; in Syria, where he lived subsequently, he embraced the Gnostic heresies; at the
time when Irenæus was preparing his work aimed
against this school, i. e. about 177, Tatian does not
appear to have been living. Comp. Iren. adv. hær.
1 : 28. Tatian can not have written his celebrated
apologetic work, Addresses to the Heathen, before

his teacher's death (166), but he may have done so soon after. In all probability, however, he had prepared the Diatessaron still earlier.

NOTE 27, p. 46. — See epist. 151 ad Algasiam quæst. 5. Theophilus . . . qui quatuor evangelistarum in unum opus dicta compingens ingenii sui nobis monimenta reliquit, hæc super hac parabola [the one respecting the Unjust Steward] in suis commentariis locutus est.

NOTE 28, p. 47. — See Euseb. Histor. Eccles. iv. 29.

NOTE 29, p. 47. — See Theodoret. hæret. fab. i. 20.

NOTE 30, p. 47. — Jerome, in the passage already cited, as well as elsewhere (in his Catalogus de Viris Illustribus), alludes to Theophilus as the author of a commentary on the Gospel (a term applied, according to the usage of that time, to the four Gospels co-ordinated into a single narrative), and even makes use of it in explaining the parable of the Unjust Steward; it is very probable, therefore, that this commentary was bound up with the Gospels.

NOTE 31, p. 52. — Hegesippus wrote a history of the church, coming down to Eleutheros, bishop of Rome, who is generally thought to have been

in office from 177 to 193.   Eusebius has made
extensive use of this work (iv. 8 and 22) in preparing his own history, and gives its author great
credit for the reliability of all his statements, and
for his doctrinal soundness (iv. 21).   In addition
to the fragments which Eusebius has preserved, we
possess another statement respecting Hegesippus,
taken by Photius from Stephanus Gobarus, a mono-
physite living at the close of the sixth century, and
incorporated in his Bibliotheca, No. 232, Bekker's
edition, p. 288.   In the fragments of Stephanus
Gobarus, we read, in connection with the quotation, " Eye hath not seen nor ear heard, neither
have entered into the heart of man the things
which God hath prepared for them that love him,"
that Hegesippus declared that this was a vain and
meaningless saying, and that all such passages are
in contradiction to the sacred scripture and to the
words of the Lord, " Blessed are the eyes which
see the things that ye see, and the ears that hear the
things that ye hear."   From this passage in Stephanus Gobarus it is not clear against whom or
against what false doctrine Hegesippus's animad-
version was directed.   It is most probable that he
aimed chiefly at a docetic error respecting the per
son of Christ.   As Paul quoted the words cited
above, from 1 Cor. ii. 9, either from Isaiah lxiv. 3
and 4, or, as Origen supposed, from an apocryphal
book known by the name of Elias, it became the
belief of certain theologians that Hegesippus in-

tended to reject the Epistles of Paul, and to condemn the validity of his doctrine. Nor did they hesitate to go further, and grant that, admitting that the passage in Corinthians was a free quotation from Isaiah, they should have to reject that as well. They even went so far as to bring Eusebius under suspicion, and to hint that he had willfully perverted ecclesiastical history.

NOTE 32, p. 52.— The apocalyptic, ethical work, known as the "Shepherd," had quotations neither from the Old nor from the New Testament; there is no lack of references in it, however.

NOTE 33, p. 53.— See, for example, · chap. 35 : "While we put away from us all injustice and wickedness, avarice, contention, cunning and deceit, slander and calumny, blasphemy, pride and self-seeking, ambition and vanity : for they who do such things are displeasing to God, and not alone they who do them, but they that have pleasure in them who do them." Comp. Rom. i. 29, et seq.

NOTE 34, p. 53.— In chap. 46: "Woe to that man: it were better for him if he had not been born, than that he should offend one of my chosen ones : it were better that a millstone were hanged about his neck and he were cast into the sea, than that he should offend one of my little ones." These

words are cited expressly on the " saying of our
Lord ; " they disclose, however, much more clearly
the very phrase taken from his lips and repeated
in the apostle's tradition, than the use of the similar passages in Matt. xxvi. 24 ; xviii. 6 ; and Luke
xvii. 2.

NOTE 35, p. 56. — " That which is born of the
flesh is flesh, and that which is born of the Spirit is
spirit. . . . The wind bloweth where it listeth,
and thou hearest the sound thereof, but canst not
tell whence it cometh or whither it goeth.   So is
every one that is born of the Spirit."

NOTE 36, p. 56. — " For every one that doeth
evil hateth the light, neither cometh to the light,
lest his deeds should be reproved."

NOTE 37, p. 62. — So, for example, Niedner's
History of the Christian Church, p. 206 : " The
first, the greater, at the time of Antoninus Pius, in
138 or 139 ; the second, the smaller, under Marcus
Aurelius, soon after 161."   The same statement is
made by Neander (Gen. Hist. of the Christ. Rel.
and Chur., 3d ed. i. 1, p. 364, et sq.) : " Since in the
superscription he does not speak of M. Aurelius as
Cæsar, it is probable that it was written before his
promotion to the imperial dignity, which took
place in 139."   Thereupon he alludes to the " greater
difficulty " which the determination of the time

when the shorter Apology was written cost him,
and states that he could come to no decision respecting it.

Note 38, p. 62. — The passage (i. 46) runs, "In
order that it may not be said in senseless perversion of what I have stated respecting Christ's being born under Quirinus 150 years ago, his teaching what may be called his system under Pontius
Pilate, and the inference which might be drawn
that all men born before his time were free from
guilt, I will meet this matter at the very outset."
Every one can see in these round numbers, and in
this mode of expression, how little the writer
meant to assign a definite date to the composition
of the Apology. Still, the year 147 is the one
which, according to our ordinary computation, is
assigned as the date when it was written. That
in the Apology of Marcion the subject is alluded
to as one occupying the public mind, has no vital
relation to the time which we have specified, although to the statement of Irenæus that Marcion
was in Rome with Cerdo at the time of Hyginus
(generally set between 137 and 141), must be
added that of the Arabic biographers of Mani, according to which Marcion came into notice in the
first year of Antoninus Pius, 138 : for the year
139 can not be coupled with this event. That
Justin cites in the Apology his work against Marcion ("and the Marcionites" does not appear in

in the title), is said without truth. For in i. 26
he alludes to his work "Against all Heresies," not
to that "Against Marcion;" the latter is cited by
Irenæus, iv. 6 : 2, after a citation of the first-named
work of Jerome in the catalogue. One circumstance opposed to this is not to be overlooked. If,
with the pushing back of the first Apology to the
year 147, the connection of the second and the
first be insisted on, and the latter is regarded as a
mere appendix to the former, the assigning of so
early a date to the former becomes the more improbable from the fact that Justin alludes in the
same to the persecutions of Crescens following him
even to his death. This seems to me to give more
decisive evidence *against* the connection of the
two, than the existing reference in the second to
what is said in the first does *for* that connection.

NOTE 39, p. 62. — If the freedom be taken to
come from this date down to 150, there is an equal
right to go back several years before 147.

NOTE 40, p. 63. — By way of illustration, we
may cite the passage which is given three times
in the Dialogue (chaps. 76, 120 and 140), "They
shall come from the east and from the west, and
shall sit down in the kingdom of heaven with
Abraham and Isaac and Jacob; but the children
of the kingdom shall be cast out into outer darkness." This coincides literally with Matt. viii. 11

and 12, excepting that in the latter we have the reading "many shall come." In like manner in the Dialogue (chap. 107) we have, "It is written in the Memorabilia, that your country folk asked him and said, 'Show us a sign.' And he answered them, 'An evil and an adulterous generation seeketh after a sign, and there shall no sign be given them but the sign of the prophet Jonas.'" This reply of the Lord coincides literally with Matt. xii. 40, with the mere use of "them" for "it."

NOTE 41, p. 63.—Respecting Luke xxii. 44, it runs, for instance, that Justin alludes in the Dialogue (chap. 103) to the sweat which ran down in great drops while Jesus was on the mount of Olives, and, indeed, it is stated with express reference to the "Memorabilia composed by his apostles and their companions." Twice (chaps. 76 and 100) he cites as a saying of the Lord: "The Son of man must suffer many things, and be rejected by the scribes and Pharisees (chap. 100, 'by the Pharisees and scribes'), and be crucified, and on the third day rise again." This agrees more closely with Mark viii. 31 and Luke ix. 21, than with Matthew xvi. 21; only in Justin the reading is the "Pharisees" instead of the "elders and high priest" (as in Matt., Mark, and Luke), and in like manner "be crucified" instead of "be slain."

NOTE 42, p. 63.—Among these is Theodoret's

Hæret. Fab. ii. 2, according to which that which is said everywhere else respecting the Gospel of the Hebrews is asserted to have been in use among the Nazaræans. Eusebius reports (Hist. Eccl. vi. 12) the judgment of Serapion, bishop of Antioch, regarding this matter. The latter found the most of it conformable to the true faith, but detected here and there something superadded even in the sense of the Docetes, which he ascribed to the influence of that community in Rhossus in Cilicia, where he found the book in use. Origen, in his comment on Matt. xiii. 54, et sq., states that, like the work of James, this reports the "brethren of Jesus" to be children of Joseph by a former marriage.

NOTE 43, p. 64. — A few examples may illustrate the character of the argument between Justin and the Clementine Homilies. Both Justin and the psuedo-Clement concur in this: "Let your yea be yea and your nay nay; whatever is more than this cometh of evil." In Matthew, however, it stands thus: "But let your communication be yea, yea, and nay, nay; for whatsoever is more than this cometh of evil." The first of these forms coincides, however, almost literally with that which is found in James v. 12, "But let [ἤτω, Justin and the pseudo-Clement ἔστω] your yea be yea, and your nay, nay." Further, we have in Justin, i. Apol. chap. 16, "Not all who say unto me, Lord, Lord, shall come into the kingdom of heaven, but they that do the will of my Father who is in heaven. For he who heareth me and doeth what I say, he heareth him that sent me." In the Homilies (8 : 7) it runs, "Jesus said to one who often called him Lord but did none of his commandments, 'Why callest thou me Lord, Lord, and doest not what I say?'" Herewith compare Matt. vii. 21, "Not every one that saith unto me Lord, Lord, shall enter into the kingdom of heaven; but he that doeth the will of my Father which is in heaven." In like manner, Luke x. 16, "He that heareth you heareth me; and he that despiseth you despiseth me; and he that despiseth me despiseth him that sent me." For the last clause the Cambridge Codex, with three old Latin manuscripts, offers the reading, "But he who heareth me, heareth him who sent me." Another well accredited reading of the greatest antiquity adds to the standard version the words, "And he that heareth me, heareth him that sent me." They take out, however, from Justin (and the Homilies) the phrase, " and doeth what I say," in order to show a reference to some other source. Two other examples which illustrate this matter will be found in the following note.

NOTE 44, p. 65. — It is very doubtful whether from the way in which Justin cites Matt. xi. 27, and especially in view of the transposition, we are right in forming conclusions as to a source different from the Gospel of the church, in spite of the close resemblance between the Homilies and Justin's citation. The passage runs in Matthew, "No one knoweth (ἐπιγινώσκει, several very ancient authorities γινώσκει, but Clemens of Alexandria often, Origen often, Irenæus often, and Didymus, ἔγνω, 'knew') the Son but the Father; neither knoweth (as before) any man the Father save the Son, and he to whomsoever the Son will reveal him" (but Clemens of Alex. often, Origen often, Irenæus twice, and Tertullian, "and to whom" — Irenæus "and to them to whom" the Son may reveal him). In Justin (Dial. 100, 1st Apol. 63) we have "No one knoweth (twice 'knew') the Father save the Son, nor the Son save the Father, and those to whom the Son shall reveal him." In the Homilies xvii. 4, xviii. 4 and 13, "No one knows the Father save the Son, as also no one knoweth the Son (οἶδεν, xviii. 3, 'nor knoweth any one the Son) save the Father and they to whom the Son will reveal him.' Epiphanius has this transposition (in the fourth century) seven times in eleven citations, and twice does it occur even in Irenæus, who in a third place still has a reading which is peculiar to the Gnostics. We may notice the other details of this verse, in which very early changes of the text are unmistakable, without having to say, This is the canonical, this the heretical text. Compare in this passage my Greek Testament, eighth edition, first part.

So in Matt. xxv. 41 : "Depart (πορεύεσθε) from me, ye accursed, into everlasting fire, prepared for the devil and his angels." Justin (Dial. 76) and the pseudo-Clemens have, "Depart (ὑπάγετε) into outer darkness which the Father has prepared for the devil (pseudo-Clemens 'Satan') and his angels." Here not only has the Sinaitic Codex the same expression ὑπάγετε, but the Cambridge, which is allied to it, together with the oldest Latin witnesses, and Irenæus and Tertullian as well, have also, "which my Father has prepared for the devil and his angels."

So, too, from the passage in the Homilies xviii. 17, " Enter through the strait and narrow way, through which you will pass into life," there has been an attempt to draw an inference in favor of an extra-canonical source ; but several of the oldest witnesses to the text, among them the Sinaitic Codex, lead to the supposition that Matt. vii. 13 and 14 was read at the most remote period as follows : "for broad and wide is the way," "for strait and narrow is the way," instead of "for wide is the gate and broad is the way," "for strait is the gate and narrow is the way."

NOTE 45, p. 66. — Throughout the whole Gospel of John this exclusively Johannean designation does not appear again; it is found only in the Apocalypse xix. 13, and as the "Word of life" at the beginning of the Epistle of John Is it to be

16

expected that Justin, if he did indeed draw from John, would use this term exclusively or with marked signs of preference?

NOTE 46, p. 68. — Comp. Volkmar, Ursprung unserer Evangelien, p. 95: "Justin contains the root of that which is cited in the Gospel of John, the beholder of the Lamb (Rev. v. 12; i. 5), or rather, Justin himself appears as one of the sources in favor of the later transformations of this latest Gospel." "Much more clearly does the most exact trial reveal this: that the one who tells of the Logos follows him who teaches regarding the Logos, the post-John follows the martyr substantially in all things; and it is beyond all doubt that Justin at least never saw this new Gospel. So far as the formula is concerned, it is not only wholly possible, but even probable, yes, the one thing probable, that the one who tells of the Logos was not only really but was also recorded to have been in the school of Justin, the teacher of the Logos."

NOTE 47, p. 69. — The word $\pi\eta\varrho\grave{o}\varsigma$ has definitively and preferably the signification "blind," as the explanations in Hesychius and Suidas show; so too the whole passage, belonging here, Constitut. v. 7: 17, where the blind man of John's Gospel as well as of Justin is called ὁ ἐκ γενετῆς πηρὸς.

NOTE 48, p. 69. — In both passages Justin has

the literal expression of John ix. 1, ἐκ γενετῆς, which is almost never elsewhere used in reference to miraculous accounts of the Gospels. Justin, too, in his Apology, puts it in immediate connection with the blind, after naming the lame and the palsied. The same seems to be true, too, of the passage in the Dialogue, although the expression is capable of being connected with the deaf and the lame.

NOTE 49, p. 69. — The emphatic expression of John and Justin, ἐκ γενετῆς, does not appear here, but ἐγεννήθην.

NOTE 50, p. 70. — That the translation of John found a place in some of our manuscripts of the Septuagint, is no less than an evidence in favor of a primitive translation followed by Justin and John, and at variance with the text of the Seventy. Naturally Tertullian (de resurr. carn. 26) as well as Theodotus (excerpt. 62) follow John's Gospel; whereas another passage of Tertullian (de carn. Christ. 24, also adv. Marc. 3, 7, and adv. Iud. 14, both as far as "tribus ad tribum") attaches itself rather to the Apocalypse i. 7. The seventh chapter of the Epistle of Barnabas must also be brought into connection with the same passages of John.

NOTE 51, p. 70. — The form retained in our translation, "be born again," which is in accordance with the Vulgate, is literally justified by, and is

significantly recommended in the answer of Nicodemus. So, too, the explanation of the new birth
made by Jesus, in the fifth verse, to Nicodemus, is
much more closely allied with being " born again "
than with being born "from above." Many com-
mentators, however, ancient as well as modern,
prefer the expression "from above." If, however,
this reading is to be taken in the sense as if the
expression of Justin did not conform to that of
John, and therefore discloses another origin than
John's Gospel, it is singularly thought possible to
decide how Justin was obliged to understand
John's expression. But see the next note.

NOTE 52, p. 71. — In order to deny the connection of the Justinian quotation with the passage
from John, it has been asserted that the expression
used in the first, the "kingdom of heaven" (βασι-
λεία τῶν οὐρανῶν), is not Johannean. But the same
expression is so strongly authenticated in the following fifth verse, by the Sinaitic Codex, by the
Docetes in Hippolytus, by a newly discovered fragment of Irenæus (in Harvey, p. 498), by the apostolical constitutions, and by Origen (in the Interpres), that it must be regarded as in the original.
(Accepted in 1864 in my synopsis.) I must remark
in addition, that the fragment of Irenæus has ἀνα-
γεννηθῇ (born again) instead of John's γεννηθῇ : it
shows how much it lay at heart with Justin and oth-

ers to give the idea of John's γεννηθῇ ἄνωθεν (born anew) by ἀναγεννηθῆτε (born again).

NOTE 53, p. 71. — For this view is claimed the similarity, also, which the quotation in the pseudo-Clementines, xi. 26, has with that of Justin : "for thus says the prophet, 'Verily I say unto you, except ye be born again with living water in the name of the Father, ye can not come into the kingdom of heaven.'" The significance of this similarity is to be inferred from what has been expressed in the previous notes. That the earlier expressly denied dependence on John's Gospel is to be discerned in the newly discovered close of his Homilies, may be seen further on. Compare what is said under the head "Naasenians."

NOTE 54, p. 72. — John uses the expression "kingdom of God" only in iii. 3; it is often met, on the contrary, in Luke, both in the Gospel and the Acts; often, too, in Mark, and several times in Matthew.

NOTE 55, p. 73. — See Dialogue, chap. 103. In the Latin version the passage runs, "in commentariis quos ab eius apostolis et eorum sectatoribus scriptos dico."

NOTE 56, p. 76. — In the same sense the passage in the fifth chapter of the Epistle to the Philadel-

phians appears to have authoritative weight: " while
I curse myself before the Gospel, as the body of
Jesus, and before the apostles as the elders of the
church. But the prophets we will love because
they have prophesied of the Gospel and have hoped
and waited for the Lord." By the expression the
" Gospel as the body of Jesus," in its connection
with the apostles and prophets, is probably to be
meant the written Gospel in the hands of the
church.

NOTE 57, p. 79.—See my Notitia editionis cod. Sin.
cum catalogo codicum, etc., p. 58 et sq. The MS. of
the Gospels indicated under No. 2, in my collection
of Greek MSS. dating probably from the ninth century, contains in three passages of Matthew the
parallels of the Hebrews' Gospel (called τὸ ἰουδαϊκόν).
At Matt. iv. 5, we have " to Jerusalem," not " into
the holy city." At xvi. 17 is the reading υἱὲ ἰωάννου
(son of John), not βαριωνᾶ (son of Jona). At xviii.
22, in the Hebrews' Gospel, after the words "seventy
times seven," the addition, "for in the prophets,
too, after that they were anointed with the Holy
Ghost, was sin found" (literally the " word of
sin," λόγος ἁμαρτίας). This remarkable passage was
given by Jerome in the Latin form. At xxvi. 74,
it is asserted that instead of the words "then he
began to curse and to swear," the Hebrews' Gospel reads, " and he denied and swore and cursed."
Such a parallelizing of special passages as we find

here would be irrational, yes, impossible, had the
Hebrews' Gospel not the same character, the same
tone, and in the main the same language, with that
of Matthew. And if some of the patristic quotations
from it do not seem to give special support to this
view, it is not to be forgotten that these citations
must be made where there are deviations from
Matthew's reading, and that they are represented
to us as such.

NOTE 58, p. 81. — See adv. hær. iii. **11 : 7.**
" Tanta est autem circa evangelia hæc firmitas, ut
et ipsi hæretici testimonium reddant eis, et ex ipsis
egrediens unusquisque eorum conetur suam con-
firmare doctrinam."

NOTE 59, p. 83. — Irenæus iii. 4 : 3 (and following him Eusebius iv. 11) makes him come to
Rome at the time of Hippolytus, between 137 and
141.

NOTE 60, p. 84. — See adv. hær. iii. **11 : 7.** Hi
autem qui a Valentino sunt, eo (sc. evangelio) quod
est secundum Johannem plenissime utentes ad os-
tensionem conjugationum suarum, ex ipso detegen-
tur nihil recte dicentes, quemadmodum ostendimus
in primo libro.

NOTE 61, p. 84. — See adv. hær. i. 8 : 5. Adhuc
autem Johannem discipulum domini docent pri-

mam Ogdoadem et omnium generationem signifi casse ipsis dictionibus, etc.

NOTE 62, p. 85. — See Philosophum. vi. 35. Liter ally the passage runs: Therefore all the prophets, and the law spoken of as Demiurgos, a foolish god, sunk in folly and ignorance (ἐλάλησαν ἀπὸ τοῦ δημιουργοῦ . . . μωροὶ οὐδὲν εἰδότες). On this account, according to Valentine, the Saviour says, " All that before me," etc.

NOTE 63, p. 85. — Appeal is made especially to i. 8 : 1–4, and 8 : 5 ; yet in the former of these only the three first Gospels are referred to, in the latter only the last; moreover, they are alluded to only by Ptolemy, whose name is given in the Latin text ("Et Ptolemæus quidem ita;" in the Greek text these words are lacking) at the end of the account. At 8 : 1–4, however, Irenæus refers to the Valentinians, not to Valentine. Can it be said, however, that 1–4 is the master with his pupils, and that in the fifth section only the pupil is meant?

NOTE 64, p. 91. — Compare, with reference to this, the Preface.

NOTE 65, p. 91. — "Si autem non prolatum est sed a se generatum est, et simile est et fraternum et eiusdem honoris id quod est vacuum ei patri, qui

prædictus est a Valentino; antiquius autem et
multo ante exsistens et honorificentius reliquis æon-
ibus ipsius Ptolemæi et Heracleonis, et reliquis omnibus qui eadem opinantur."

NOTE 66, p. 92.—ʽΟ τῆς Οὐαλεντίνου σχολῆς δοκι-
μώτατος is the expression of Clemens.

NOTE 67, p. 92.—Τὸν Οὐαλεντίνου λεγόμενον εἶναι
γνώριμον ʽΗρακλέωνα.

NOTE 68, p. 92.— Comp. Orig. contr. Cels. 5.
ὅ Μαρκίωνος γνώριμος Ἀπελλῆς, αἱρέσεώς τινος γενόμε-
νος πατήρ, and the Tert. de carn. Chr. 1. "Apelles discipulus et postea desertor ipsius" (id est,
Marcionis)ⅰ Psuedo-Tertull. de præscr. hæret. LI.
"Apelles discipulus Marcionis qui . . . postea . . .
a Marcione segregatus est." Comp. also Hippol.
Philosoph. vii. 12.

NOTE 69, p. 92.— But is the real meaning of
Κέρδων διαδέχεται ʽΗρακλέωνα, Cerdo follows Herakleon? Is it not rather, Cerdo follows in my work on
Herakleon? If any one should happen to be pleased
with this burlesque style of exposition, he will
scarcely be able to persuade others of its excellence.
Another discovery on the same side deserves equal
credit. Hippolytus alludes to a contention between the two wings of the Valentinian school in
these words: "The adherents of the Italiotic fac-

tion, to which Herakleon and Ptolemy belong, say thus; the adherents of the oriental faction, to which Axionikus and Bardesanes belong, thus." "Over this," he goes on to say, "they, and any body else who likes to, may quarrel." From this the inference is to be drawn not only that this "they" relates specifically to the above-mentioned heads of factions, but the word ζητείτωσαν, "may quarrel," indicates that these persons were still living and contending at the time of Hippolytus. Who could doubt after applying this test that Marcion and Tertullian were contemporaries, since the latter writes, de carne Chr.: "On such grounds hast thou probably ventured to put out of the way so many original writings respecting Christ, Marcion, in order to disprove his existence in the flesh. On what authority hast thou done this? I ask. If thou art a prophet, then prophesy; if an apostle, preach openly; if a follower of the apostles, hold fast to them; and if thou art a Christian, believe what is transmitted to us. But if thou art none of these, I might rightly say, then die, for thou art already dead; for thou canst not be a Christian if thou hast not the faith which makes one such."

NOTE 70, p. 93. — See Euseb. Hist. Eccl. iv. 7: φησὶν (Agrippa Castor) αὐτὸν εἰς μὲν τὸ εὐαγγέλιον τέσσαρα πρὸς τοῖς εἴκοσι συντάξαι βιβλία. Even if nothing more definite is to be determined respecting the book of Basilides, it is a fact of weight that Agrip-

pa Castor had already made use of the same expression, from which we learn with certainty that
some centuries later he indicated the collective
character of our Gospels.

NOTE 71, p. 96. — When the apostles were ask-
ing whether it is better not to marry, the story is
that the Lord answered : "Not all can understand
this, for there are eunuchs who are so from their
birth, others are compelled to be so, and others
still have made themselves eunuchs for the everlasting kingdom's sake." The last words are sup-
plemented by what is found in Clemens. In like
manner the same expression is cited by the Niko-
laites in Epiphanius 25 : 6. Another extract found
in Clemens "from the 23d book of the Exegetica
of Basilides," contains no passage to be compared
with this, nor does that in the Archelaus-disputa-
tion.

NOTE 72, p. 96. — On this account he says, "Do
not throw your pearls before swine, nor give that
which is holy to the dogs."

NOTE 73, p. 96. — That Jerome (in the pref. to
Matt. and likewise in his translation of the first
Homily of Origen on Luke, according to Jerome,
also, Ambrosius on Luke) mentions an original Gospel of Basilides, probably rests only upon the acceptance of the 24 books of the Gospel as of a Gospel

in a certain sense apocryphal; we must therefore
consider the secret communications of Matthew,
which according to Hippolytus were extolled by
Basilides and his followers, as that Gospel of Basilides.

Note 73, p. 96.—See vii. 25. "As it is written,
'And the creation itself groaneth and travaileth
together, waiting for the manifestation of the children of God.'" (Rom. viii. 22 and 19.) "That is
the . . . wisdom of which he says the Scripture
asserts, 'Not with words which human wisdom
teacheth, but which the Spirit teacheth.'"   1 Cor.
ii. 13. Reference is made to the same in Eph. iii.
3 and 5, and 2 Cor. xii. 4.

Note 74, p. 96.—See vii. 26. "That is it, he
says, which is written: 'The Holy Ghost shall
come upon thee, . . . and the power of the Highest
shall overshadow thee.'" The allusion to Matthew
is in vii. 22, and relates to the account of the star
seen by the wise men.

Note 75, p. 96.—See vii. 20. "Basilides, therefore, and Isodorus, Basilides' own son and disciple,
assert that Matthias transmitted to them certain secret communications which he had received
from the Saviour as a special charge. We shall
see how openly Basilides as well as Isodorus and
their whole crowd of followers calumniate not only

Matthias but the Saviour also." This is at the commencement of his representation of Basilides and his school. And just so often as he has occasion, in what follows, to mention Basilides, he is to be understood as alluded to in the same strain as at the outset.

NOTE 76, p. 98.— See Theodoret. Quæst. xlix. in libr. iv. Regum: " On this account I believe that the Ophites are called Naassenians." The only mention of the Ophites in Hippolytus is viii. 20 : *Εἰ δὲ καὶ ἕτεραί τινες αἱρέσεις ὀνομάζονται Καϊνῶν, Ὀφιτῶν ἢ Νοαχαϊτῶν (Νοαχιτῶν?) καὶ ἑτέρων τοιούτων οὐκ ἀναγκαῖον ἥγημαι τὰ ὑπ᾿ αὐτῶν λεγόμενα ἢ γινόμενα ἐκθέσθαι,* etc. From this there can scarcely any inference be drawn, except that to Hippolytus the name of Ophites seemed quite secondary compared with that of Naassenians.

NOTE 77, p. 99. — The same division of the sentence is followed by many of our oldest textual documents, namely, the oldest patristic extracts.

NOTE 78, p. 100. — We do not add to t e above all the peculiar Gnostic explanations appended to the passages in the original.

NOTE 79, p. 100. — In connection with these extracts we must call particular attention to the fact that they quite often unite a free transposition

of the text with a strictly close repetition of the
words. They reveal in this a striking similarity to
the citations of Justin. The same kind of quotations from Matthew and the other synoptic Gospels
compel us to draw an immediate inference as to an
extra-canonical source. Does not the analogy with
these Gnostic and almost contemporaneous extracts from John show how little such a hasty conclusion as to the Justinian citation is justified?
Or are we, in the case of the quotation given above
from John vi. 53, to draw a conclusion as to that
extra-canonical source, because, in entire analogy
with Justin's quotation from John vi. 51, the concluding words, " ye shall not enter the kingdom of
heaven," are given instead of John's "you have
no life in you " ?

NOTE 80, p. 102. — With reference to this, see
a previous note. Tertullian adv. Marcion, i. 19,
writes: Cum igitur sub Antonino primus Marcion
hunc deum induxerit. . . . The determination of
dates in Marcion's works is a matter presenting
the gravest difficulties. Although the "invaluit
sub Aniceto" of Irenæus iii. 4:3 is not to be applied to his appearance at Rome, yet there is a
contradiction still remaining involving a statement
of Clemens (Strom. vii. 17), who places Marcion
before Basilides and Valentine. As the latter
position appears to be sustained by the recent
striking discovery of a memorandum of Philastrius

(hær. 45, qui, i. e. Marcion, devictus atque fuga-
tus a beato Johanne evangelista), . . . so the same
appears to be corroborated by the recent exhuming
of the unquestionably ante-Jerome prologue to
John, of which I shall have occasion to speak when
I come to the Papias problem. Manifestly we
have to deal with a primitive tradition running
back to a time antedating Marcion's earliest activity and his removal to Rome.

NOTE 81, p. 103. — See Iren. iii. 2 and 12, where
the assertion is made by the heresiarchs with
specific reference to Marcion : Dicentes se . . . sin-
ceram invenisse veritatem. Apostolos enim admis-
cuisse ea quæ sunt legalia Salvatoris verbis. (iii.
2 : 2.) Et apostolos quidem adhuc quæ sunt Judæorum sentientes annuntiasse evangelium, se autem sinceriores et prudentiores apostolis esse.
Unde et Marcion et qui ab eo sunt ad intercidendas conversi sunt scripturas, quasdam quidem in
totum non cognoscentes, secundum Lucam autem
evangelium et epistolas Pauli decurtantes, hæc
sola legitima esse dicunt quæ ipsi minoraverunt.
(iii. 12 : 12.) Similar words in Tert. adv. Marc. iv. 3.
Sed enim Marcion nactus epistolam Pauli ad Galatas,
etiam ipsos apostolos suggilantis ut non recto pede
incedentes ad veritatem evangelii, simul et accu-
santis pseudapostolos quosdam pervertentes evangelium Christi, connititur ad destruendum statum
eorum evangeliorum, quæ propria et sub apostolo-

rum nomine edantur vel etiam apostolicorum, ut
scilicet fidem quam illis adimit suo conferat.

Note 82, p. 104. — See Iren. iii. 1 : 1 (also Euseb. Hist. Eccl. v. 8) : Et Lucas autem, sectator Pauli, quod ab illo prædicabatur evangelium in libro
condidit. Tert. adv. Marc. iv. 5. Nam et Lucæ
digestum Paulo adscribere solent. In like manner Orig. in Euseb. Hist. Eccl. vi. 25 ; Eus. iii. 4 and
Hier. de viris illustrib. cap. 7 : in all these three
passages the assertion is distinctly made that it
was then understood that Paul indicated Luke's
Gospel when he spoke of *his* Gospel. Rom. ii. 16.
Here belongs also Ps.-Orig. Dial. contr. Marcionit.,
sect. i. (Or. opp. ed. Delarue, vol. i. p. 808), where, to
the question of the Orthodox man who asks, "Who
wrote the Gospel of which thou sayest that it is the
only one?" the Marcionite replies, "Christ," and
to the second question, "Did the Lord himself
write 'I was crucified and rose again on the third
day'?" the answer is, "*That* was added by the
apostle Paul."

Note 83, p. 105. — See A. Ritschl (Prof. at
Gottingen) in the Jahrb. f. deutsch. Theol. 1866, 2.
p. 355 : so is he (i. e. Prof. Tischendorf) unable
naturally to convince himself that in a remote
province like Pontus there could not be without a
degree of personal fault a more limited acquaint-

ance with Christian books than in other provinces
of the church.

NOTE 84, p. 105. — Had the Gospel of John appeared in Gottingen or in some other celebrated
University-city of Germany, I should have been
more able to take this charge home to myself.

NOTE 85, p. 106. — See Iren. i. 27 : 2 : Et super
hæc id, quod est secundum Lucam evangelium cir-
cumcidens etc. III. 12 : 12 : Unde et Marcion et
qui ab eo sunt . . . secundum Lucam autem evangelium et epistolas Pauli decurtantes. Tertull.
adv. Marcion, iv. 2 : Ex iis quos habemus Lucam
videtur Marcion elegisse quem cæderet. Porro
Lucas non apostolus sed apostolicus. . . Ibid, iv.
4 : Quod ergo pertinet ad evangelium interim Lucæ, quatenus communio eius inter nos et Marcionem de veritate disceptat, adeo antiquius est quod
est secundum nos. . . Si enim id evangelium quod
Lucæ refertur, penes nos (viderimus an et penes
Marcionem) ipsum est quod Marcion per antitheses
suas arguit, ut interpolatum a protectoribus Judais-
mi . . . utique non potuisset arguere nisi quod in-
venerat. Epiph. hær. xlii. 11.

NOTE 86, p. 108. — See Tertull. adv. Marc. iv.
2 : Marcion evangelio scilicet suo nullum adscribit
auctorem. . . .

17

NOTE 87, p. 108. — See a previous note.

NOTE 88, p. 112. — See adv. Marc. iv. 5: Cur non hæc quoque (cætera evangelia) Marcion attigit, aut emendanda si adulterata, aut agnoscenda si integra? Nam et competit ut, si qui evangelium pervertebant, eorum magis curarent perversionem quorum sciebant auctoritatem receptiorem. Likewise, De carne Chr. 2: Rescindendo quod retro credidisti, sicut et ipse confiteris in quadam epistola. Directly before this we have, however, Tot originalia instrumenta Christi, Marcion, delere ausus es.

NOTE 89, p. 113. — See De carne Chr. 2, in the previous note; see also adv. Marc. iv. 4.

NOTE 90, p. 113. — See adv. Marc. iv. 4. Quid si nec epistolam agnoverint?

NOTE 91, p. 113. — See Ritschl in Jahrb. für deutshe Theol. i. a. l. "The African was, however, great in his malicious perversion of the assertions of his heretical opponents, and whoever has followed the course of his onslaught upon Marcion must know how much he had to draw from Tertullian's expression, in order to establish the historical fact which he wanted to make good. If Marcion complained of the depravatio evangelii and gave himself out as the emendator evangelii, he meant by evangelium the regula fidei, Christianity as a common belief, which he wanted to purify from the Judaic additions made by the anti-Pauline school. And since Marcion did not defend the Gospel canon which was known to Tertullian, the latter drew the inference that he was opposing the value of this collection on the ground of being a reformer of it.

NOTE 92, p. 114. — See adv. Marc. iv. 4: Emendator sane evangelii (this is consequently Tertullian's own statement, from which there is an effort to prove his misunderstanding of the matter) a Tiberianis usque ad Antoniana tempora everti Marcion solus et primus obvenit, exspectatus tam diu a Christo, pœnitente iam quod apostolos præmisisse properasset sine præsidio Marcionis; nisi quod humanæ temeritatis, non divinæ auctoritatis negotium est hæresis, quæ sic semper emendat evangelia dum vitiat.

NOTE 93, p. 114. — *Τὸν μὲν παράκλητον Μοντανὸν αυχοῦντες.*

NOTE 94, p. 118.— Alii vero ut donum spiritus frustrentur, quod in novissimis temporibus secundum placitum patris effusum èst in humanum genus, illam speciem (the account of the " quadriforme evangelium " went before, to whose four " species " there is a subsequent reference) non ad-

mittunt quæ est secundum Johannis evangelium,
in qua paracletum se missurum dominus promisit;
sed simul et evangelium et propheticum repellunt
spiriṭum.   Infelices vere qui pseudoprophetas (a
better reading assuredly than pseudoprophetæ)
quidem esse volunt, propheticam vero gratiam
repellunt ab ecclesia; similia patientes his, qui
propter eos qui in hypocrisi veniunt etiam a fra-
trum communicatione se abstinent.

Note 95, p. 118. — Otherwise the Montanists
and their most decided followers must have met in
their rejection of the Gospel of John.   There is
not only no support for this view, involving as it
does the grossest contradictions, but it contradicts
as well what Hippolytus, Tertullian, and Eusebius
have recorded respecting the connection of the
Paraclete with the Montanist prophetic spirit.
And had the Montanists thrown away the Gospel
of John at the outset, how would it be clear that
in Tertullian, the reformer of Montanism, we find
(without the least trace of a contrast to the earlier
Montanism) the Gospel of John standing in the
closest connection with Montanism?   Besides, all
which is expressed in the passage of Irenæus applies just as appositely to the opponents of Montanism, as it is inapposite and incomprehensible
when it is made to refer to the Montanists.

Note 96, p. 119. — Neander (Hist. of the Chris-

tian Church, 1856, 3d ed.) remarks in allusion to
the Irenæus passage, which he understands just as
I do : "Irenæus, from whom we receive our first
knowledge respecting this party [the Alogians], assuredly says too much when he states that they
rejected the Gospel of John in consequence of the
passage relating to the Paraclete. That passage
alone certainly could not have led to this, for they
only made use of it, as was the case with others,
to limit it to the apostles, in order to take away
the support from beneath the Montanists. But
since they, if those words of Christ were brought
against them with a Montanist interpretation, stig-
matized the whole document which contained them
as not genuine, the inference was a quick one that,
in consequence of a kind of legerdemain only too
common in theological discussion, they had in
consequence of this passage rejected the whole
Gospel."

Note 97, p. 119. — Adv. Prax. 13, he says : Nos
paracleti, non hominum discipuli. Comp. further
De resurrect. carn. 63 (per novam prophetiam de
paracleto inundantem), and many other passages.

Note 98, p. 120. — Irenæus states (iii. 3 : 4)
that the story was repeated after Polycarp that
John once encountered Cerinth while bathing, but
instantly left the bath with these words, " Let us
get out ; the bath might come to pieces with such

an enemy to truth in it as Cerinth is." That two hundred years later Epiphanius attributed this anecdote to "Ebion" has no weight when set over against the authority of Irenæus. For the statement of Epiphanius (hær. 28 : 2) that Cerinth once had communication with Peter, and that he was one of those who criticised his relations with the Gentile centurion Cornelius, there is no earlier voucher.

NOTE 99, p. 123. — According to 2 : 27, Celsus suffers his Jews to be told that Christians changed and corrupted the "Gospel" for polemic ends.

NOTE 100, p. 127.—Mary, poor, living by the work of her own hands, is said to have been driven away by her husband, a carpenter, in consequence of an adulterous connection with a soldier named Panthera; and the story is that Jesus hired himself in Egypt in consequence of his poverty, and learned secret arts there.

NOTE 101, p. 127. — See Origen 2 : 13, where the Jew of Celsus says, "I might bring forward many things which were written of Jesus, and which are strictly true, though differing from the writings of the disciples; yet I will leave this on one side."

NOTE 102, p. 128. — See Der Ursprung unserer Evangelien, p. 80.

NOTE 103, p. 126. —*Εἰ μὲν οὖν οὐκ ἔγραψεν.*

NOTE 104, p. 129.—*Εἰ δὲ κἀκεῖνον ἀρξάμενος συνετέλεσε.*

NOTE 105, p. 130. — That there is an allusion to the Marcionites does not do violence to this determination of the date; still, mention is made of the heresy of Marcion as early as the first Apology of Justin.

NOTE 106, p. 132.—In 1851 appeared in the Hague a prize essay written by me in 1849: De evangelior. apocryph. origine et usu. I hope to publish a revised edition of it for the use of learned readers.

NOTE 107, p. 134.— Those who care to go further into this matter I must beg to see in the original Greek how the passage runs in Justin, in Luke (i. 30 et sq.), and in the Protevangel (see my elaborately annotated Evang. Apocr. 1853, p. 21 et sq. Protevang. chap. xi.).

NOTE 108, p. 134. — Justin has it: The Spirit of the Lord shall come upon thee and the power of the Highest shall overshadow thee; therefore that which shall be born of thee is holy, the Son of God. Luke says: The Holy Ghost shall come upon thee, and the power of the Highest shall overshadow thee; therefore also that holy thing which shall be born of thee shall be called the Son of God. The pseudo-James has it thus: For the power of the Lord shall overshadow thee; therefore shall the holy thing which is born of thee be called the Son of the Highest.

NOTE 109, p. 135. — In Justin it runs: Πίστιν δὲ καὶ χαρὰν λαβοῦσα . . . ἀπεκρίνατο. In the pseudo-James: Χαρὰν δε λαβοῦσα Μαριὰμ ἀπίει πρὸς Ἐλισά-βετ.

NOTE 110, p. 135. — See Hilgenfeld : Kritische Untersuchungen über die Evangelien Justins, p. 159 et sq.

NOTE 111, p. 136. — See Epiph. hæres. xxvi. 12.

NOTE 112, p. 137. — Would one accept a closer relation between the Protevangelium and the Gnostic book of Mary, there would be a certain probability in giving the heretical Gnostic production such a dependence upon the half-Catholic book of James as is manifested in the many instances of extra-ecclesiastical literature depending upon that of the church. The hints given by Augustine in the twenty-third book against Faustus would also have weight in this regard, while those too of the Gnostic work called De generatione Mariæ have similar value. Mary was represented in this as

a daughter of a priest Joachim of the tribe of
Levi.

NOTE 113, p. 137.— See Orig. opp. ed. Delarue,
iii. 463 (comm. in Matt. tom. x. 17).

NOTE 114; p. 138.— For a full characterization
of this matter, the passage from Hilgenfeld may
have so much appositeness as to admit of its being
quoted. "It is certainly true that the present
form of the Protevangel, while alluding to John
and his parents without describing his birth more
closely, is incomplete, and indicates more than it
tells; but since the Gnostics in their Γέννα Μαρίας
gave an account of the dumbness which came upon
Zacharias, the suspicion is not risked that the
primitive draft of the Gospel contained an account
of those antecedent events. The suspicion may
not be ventured; it is entirely without support.
For the story of Zacharias's dumbness stands in the
Gnostic production completely isolated; it has not
the slightest analogy either with Luke or with the
Protevangel. If the latter points to something beyond itself, it is at any rate clear that our canonical Gospels, including that of Luke, stand in the
background. On the other hand, there is a close
connection established with the Gnostic primitive
form of the Protogospel: "the same is manifestly
received only in a revision, worked over after the
canonical Gospels mainly, causing it thereby to

lose, as it would seem, many of its peculiarities."
But may not then the Book of James have a like
close connection with the canonical Gospels, taking
into account the agreement with them of its whole
nature and purport? Further on, we read : "The
admission that Justin made use of such an ancient
Protevangel may be allowed if it be held as probable that such a production, bearing among the Gnostics the title Γέννα Μαρίας, contained a genealogy of
Mary." After further remarks there follows : "All
the more attractive therefore is another trace to
which Origen leads us. In the passage where he
alludes to the Gospel of Peter and the Protogospel
of James, he speaks of them both as bearing the same
testimony. But how would this be if both Gospels
should prove to be closely related? How if in
the Protogospel of James the preliminary history
of Peter's Gospel — for there can scarcely be a
doubt that there was such a preliminary history —
were accepted? Is not this more than building on
the sand?"

Note 115, p. 139. — The first reference to Justin appears, as Hilgenfeld was the first to remark,
in the document addressed to the congregations at
Lyons and Vienna about the year 177. Allusion
is made there (Eus. Hist. Eccl. v. 1 : 3, et sq.) to the
martyrdom of Zacharias. Tertullian in the Scor-
piacum contr. Gnosticos, chap. 8, refers to the same
thing, only with more definite and positive lan-

guage. Clemens Alexandr. alludes to the circumstances connected with the midwives. Strom. vii.
page 889 in Potter. Origen is the first who mentions the work as the book of James.

NOTE 116, p. 141. — We pass over the story of
the death of Zacharias in the Protevangel to Matt.
xxiii. 36. If this can be so understood as if affording an historical basis for the passage in Matthew, it would strengthen the proof of the antiquity of the Gospels which we derive from the document of James.

NOTE 117, p. 143. — A third reference must be
accepted in the thirty-eighth chapter, where he
in like manner cites Is. lxv. 2, and l. 6: "I gave
my back to the smiters and exposed my cheeks to
blows:" see also the words already cited of the
xxii. Psalm, "They cast lots," etc., in conjunction with Psalm iii. 5, "I laid me down and slept;
I awaked," etc., and Ps. xxii. 8. He makes this close
to the prophecies: "and this was all done by the
Jews to Christ, as you can learn" (here we have
this express declaration) "from the Acts compiled
under Pontius Pilate."

NOTE 118, p. 144. — Instead of ἄκτα we have
the specific word ὑπομνήματα. The same title, prepared too for the official report of Pilate, appears
in the Præsidial Acts relative to the martyrs Tara-

chus, Probus and Andronikus. See my Evv. apocr. p. lxii. In the same sense it is used in a homily inscribed to Chrysostom (Chrys. opp. tom. v. p. 942) and in the Martyrium Ignatii, chap. iii. But with this we must reconcile the expression ὑπομνηματικαὶ ἐφημερίδες, which Philo uses (de legat. ad Cajum 25) in reference to the reports which were sent by Alexander to the emperor of Rome. The oldest Latin title, found in Gregory of Tours, is the Gesta Pilati.

NOTE 119, p. 145. — The thirty-eight years and the healing on the Sabbath are taken from John's narrative, v. 2; that about the man who was carried by, from Matthew ix.

NOTE 120, p. 146. — See Weitzel: Die christliche Passahfeier der drei ersten Jahrhunderte, p. 248 et sq.

NOTE 121, p. 147. — On scientific grounds it is not to be excused if one in learned investigations follows in the old rut and speaks of the Gospel of Nicodemus. Compare my re-establishing of the old title and the investigation respecting it in the Prolegomenon of the Evangelia apocrypha, p. liv. et sq. It corresponds best with what was said above respecting the use of the word ὑπομνήματα, if we say the "Acts of Pilate." The Latin designation, Gesta Pilati, also answers well to this.

NOTE 122, p. 148. — See Euseb. Hist. Eccl. ix. 5 and 7.

NOTE 123, p. 149. — Comp. with reference to this my paper: Pilati circa Christum indicio quid lucis afferatur ex actis Pilati. Lipsiæ, 1855.

NOTE 124, p. 149. — Of later writers Epiphanius admits (hæres. L. Quartodec. i.) that appeal was made to the Acts of Pilate in order to establish the time of Jesus' death, it being given there as the twenty-fifth of March. He adds, however, that he had found copies where the eighteenth was assigned as the date. The first date is found also in our texts.

NOTE 125, p. 150. — See the two ἀναφοραὶ Πιλάτου in our Evv. apocr. pp. 413–425.

NOTE 126, p. 150. — It will gratify the wish of the reader if I insert here a portion of the text of the work itself. We select for this purpose the whole of the third chapter, tinged as it is with the coloring of John: "And full of rage Pilate came forth from the hall of judgment (the Prætorium) and said to them, 'I take the sun to witness that I find no fault in this man.' But the Jews answered and said to the governor, 'If this man had not been a malefactor, we should not have delivered him over to you.' Pilate answered, 'Take

him away and judge him after your law.' The
Jews answered, 'It is not permitted to us to put
any one to death.' Pilate said, 'Did God order
you not to put any one to death and not me as
well?' Pilate went again into the judgment hall
and called Jesus to him privately, and asked him,
'Art thou the king of the Jews?' Jesus answered
him, 'Speakest thou that of thyself, or have others
told it thee?' Pilate answered Jesus, 'Am I a
Jew? Thy people and the high priest have delivered thee over to me: what hast thou done?'
Jesus answered, 'My kingdom is not of this
world; for if my kingdom were of this world, then
would my servants have fought that I should not
be delivered over to the Jews: but now is my
kingdom not thence.' Then spoke Pilate unto
unto him, 'Thou art a king, then.' Jesus answered him, 'Thou sayest that I am a king. For
this cause was I born and am come into the world,
that every one who is out of the truth may hear
my voice.' Pilate asked, 'What is truth?' Jesus
answered, 'The truth is from heaven.' Pilate asked
again, 'Is there no truth on the earth?' Jesus
answered, 'Thou seest how those who speak the
truth are brought to judgment of those who have
power on the earth.'" At the close of the fourth
chapter we have: "But when Pilate saw the
throng of Jews around him he perceived that
many of the Jews were weeping, and said, 'Not
all the people wish him to die.' Then answered

the elders, 'We, the whole people, have come, that he might be sentenced to death.' Pilate answers them, 'Wherefore should he die?' The Jews reply, 'Because he said he was God's son and a king.'"

NOTE 127, p. 151. — Compare respecting this my Evangelia Apocrypha in the Prolegg. i. p. xxxix. et sq.

NOTE 128, p. 152. — See the same work.

NOTE 129, p. 153.— Comp. Hilgenfeld: Kritische Untersuchungen über die Evv. Justins, der Clementinischen Homilien und Marcions, 1850 (therefore before 1853), p. 387 et sq. Here an effort is ascribed to the fourth Evangelist to subordinate Peter to the beloved disciple, and on this account the fourth Evangelist's independence of Peter's Gospel is admitted, but afterwards every proof favoring the use of the Gospel of John is denied to the connection of the homilies with him. (Page 346 had thus decided with respect to the expression, Hom. 3: 52, "My sheep hear my voice": "It is a question whether the Gospel of John or one still older contained this passage.") "Against such a use," it goes on literally to say, "stands the glaring difference in the tendency of both writers, so that in presupposing an acquaintance with this Gospel one must admit a polemic objective view. Let one imagine an attack made upon the divinity of Christ, and satisfy himself how such an author could dispose of John i. 1; x. 33, et sq.; xx. 28. While, in John x. 36, Jesus declares himself substantially as the Son of God, so that his own assertion is an expression of his divinity, the author of the Homilies takes the same expression, 16 : 15, to be a decisive statement of the difference between Jesus and the Deity. The Lord never declared himself to be God, but the Son of God. How was it possible, after using the fourth Gospel, to expressly limit the time of the intercourse of Jesus and the disciples to a single year, and not, as later teachers have accepted, the time of his public career? How could he besides, while declaring Peter to be the first fruits and cherished disciple of Christ, so markedly leave out the Johannean portraiture, and among the expressions used by Jesus regarding the devil (xix. 2), which he doubtless collects as completely as was possible, how could he omit such an expression as John viii. 44? The result of our investigation is in a word this, that even in Clementine's Homilies the Gospel of Peter, in contradistinction to Justin and some farther continuations, is used; with him Matthew, perhaps Luke also, but certainly not the Gospel of John."

NOTE 130, p. 154. — With the utmost probability Celsus made use (about 150) of the epistle of Barnabas. That he specifically speaks of the apostles as πονηρότατοι, Origen infers (contr. Cels. i. 63) from the use of the epistle.

NOTE 131, p. 156. — The text however is not to be judged from what is published, nor is that of Dr. Hilgenfeld, who has contented himself with unscientifically repeating it just as it was left in the edition of two hundred years ago.

NOTE 132, p. 160. — See Beiträge i. a. l.: "These words do not suit if they be made with Orelli (Selecta pp. eccl. capita, etc.) to refer to the apocryphal fourth book of Ezra which Barnabas elsewhere cites." One would draw the inference from this which Volkmar insists should be deduced from Credner's words, quite in antagonism to what Credner himself asserts.

NOTE 133, p. 160. — See Volkmar: Index lectt. in liter. univ. Turic. 1864, page 16. Scriptum est apud Esdram Prophetam iv. Esd. viii. 3 : " multi creati, pauci autem salvati." Hoc auctor confudit cum dicto Christi apud Matth. xix. 30, (?) Christiano illo interpretamento dicti Esdrani. Quod ed. mea Esdræ Prophetæ, 1863, p. 290, post J. C. de Orelli et C. A. Crednerum (how do the words of Credner himself, cited in the previous note, agree with this?) quorum meritum plerisque in memoriam revocandum erat, demonstravit, omnibus qui hucusque de ea re ex ed. mea iudicarunt, persuasit. . . .

NOTE 134, p. 160. — See D. F. Strauss, Das Leben Jesu, p. 55.

NOTE 135, p. 160. — Volkmar (Der Ursprung unserer Evv. p. 161) assigns the date of this work to " 97, harvest time."

NOTE 136, p. 161. — The statement given above of the heathen scoffer Celsus merits unquestionable pre-eminence over this discovery; for according to him the expression, "It is easier for a camel to go through the eye of a needle than for a rich man to enter into the kingdom of God," is but another form of Plato's "It is impossible that he who is extraordinarily rich should be extraordinarily good." See Origen contr. Cels. 6:16. As for other matters, however, the crafty trickery of Volkmar does not derive any reflected credit from Renan, as it was said to do in the earlier editions of this work; it should have the claim allowed it of having anticipated Renan, since the latter work appeared in 1863, whereas Volkmar's preface to "Esdra Propheta" is dated October, 1862. Honor to whom honor is due.

NOTE 137, p. 161. — So Volkmar i. a. l. p. 161. "118–119 Alexandrine epistle named after Barnabas, with a knowledge of the Gospel of Matt. as *a new work with the most ample use of Matthew*, but with the sayings of Christ taken only from the hallowed Old Testament."

NOTE 138, p. 162. — A later affix with Matt. than with Barnabas is "to repentance."

NOTE 139, p. 162. — By this I seek to render literally ἐπεὶ οὖν μέλλουσιν λέγειν.

NOTE 140, p. 163. — Not less than in Barnabas does it become clear in Justin that he makes the brazen serpent of John's Gospel the type of the cross. Even Justin's expression, Dial. 91, appeared to have flowed from a recollection of John: Προσφεύγουσι τῷ τὸν ἐσταυρωμένον υἱὸν αὐτοῦ πέμψαντι εἰς τὸν κόσμον, for John iii. 17, οὐ γὰρ ἀπέστειλεν ὁ θεὸς τὸν υἱὸν αὐτοῦ εἰς τὸν κόσμον, is closely connected with iii. 14. Naturally, with Barnabas there is the same process of divination applied that we find earlier among the Clementines. So Volkmar i. a. l. p. 67 : The author "seems not to depend at all upon the Sap. Sal. 16 : 5, which had already prefigured the typical character of the serpent. But least of all upon the Logos Gospel (John iii. 14), for his special comparison of the lifting up of the serpent in the wilderness with the lifting up of Christ (on the cross and thus to the heaven) is wanting here : and how could one who in this connection read 'in order that every one who should believe in him should not perish, but have ever-

lasting life' discard such a saying as the above?
No one of us (!) could do it." In the same fashion
Volkmar shows in his Append. to Credner's Gesch.
des Neutest. Kanons (1860, p. 372) that Tertullian
had not been acquainted with the first Epistle of
Peter, or, if he could not deny to Tertullian acquaintance with the work Adv. Gnosticos, asserts that it
was only subsequently to 207 that he was familiar
with it. He writes, " What apt proofs it (the epistle) offers to the opponent of the Gnosis de resurr.
carn. . . . the Montanist moralist even, de pudicit.
. . . or de habitu mulier. . . . How was he able
to pass over Peter in the letter, when going
through the entire list of prophets and apostles?
An Epistola Petri has no place in his Instrumentum Apostolorum, as he draws it up in both
its chief forms." Pity that that whole course of
acute reasoning finds its answer in the fact (as Dr.
Aberle has already shown in the Theol. Quartal-
schrift, 1864, 1) that its first propounder has overlooked Tertullian's complete work, De oratione,
where (Semler, p. 15, chap. xiv.) express reference
is made to the " præscriptio Petri," in 1 Pet. iii.

NOTE 141, p. 166. — Irenæus says (hær. iii. 3: 4
and ii. 22: 5) that he lived in Trajan's day, 98 to
117. Eusebius (in the Chronicon) sets his death
at the year 100, and Jerome (de viris illustrib. and
elsewhere) 68 years after the death of Christ.

The Chronic. Pasch. has 72 years after the ascension of Christ.

NOTE 142, p. 169. — The change of arrangement in several of our oldest Itala manuscripts (Matthew, John, Luke, Mark) does not rest on a chronological basis, but, according to Tertullian, upon the connection, first of the two men who were apostles, then of those who were helpers of the apostles.

NOTE 143, p. 171. — This is in accord with the statement of Eusebius iii. 37 : 2, that already at Trajan's time (98 to 117) a part of the missionary activity inspired by Christianity consisted in the diffusion of the written gospel narratives (καὶ τὴν τῶν θείων εὐαγγελίων παραδιδόναι γραφήν).

NOTE 144, p. 171. — Λογίων κυριακῶν ἐξήγησις. Rufin, following the ancient usage, translates λόγια by oracula. It is extremely probable that the book of Papias, true to the chiliastic standpoint of the man, was largely devoted to the prophecies of the Lord. Christian usage, however, gave the word a larger significance, so that the sayings of the Lord and of the apostles, although not having the precise character of prophecy, are yet called by that name, and the Holy Writ was designated as θεῖα λόγια. Papias makes use of the same expression in conveying a notion of the contents of the Gospels of

Matthew and Mark, where the narrower conception conveyed in the word "prophecy" does not do justice to the meaning.

NOTE 145, p. 172. — *Τὰς παρὰ τοῦ κυρίου τῇ πίστει δεδομένας καὶ ἀπ' αὐτῆς παραγινομένας τῆς ἀληθείας.*

NOTE 146, p. 173. — *Τοὺς τῶν πρεσβυτέρων ἀνέκρινον λόγους, τι Ἀνδρέας ἢ τί Πέτρος εἶπεν . . . ἅ τε Ἀριστίων καί ὁ πρεσβύτ. Ἰωάνν. οἱ τοῦ κυρ. μαθηταὶ λέγουσιν.*

NOTE 147, p. 174. — *Τοὺς μὲν τῶν ἀππ. λόγους παρὰ τῶν αὐτοῖς παρηκολουθηκότων ὁμολογεῖ παρειληφέν αι, Ἀριστίωνος δὲ καὶ τοῦ πρεσβυτ. Ἰω. αὐτήκοον ἑαυτόν φησι γενέσθαι.*

NOTE 148, p. 176. — To understand who these presbyters were, it is not necessary to understand that they were personally connected with the immediate companions of the apostles, as Irenæus (iv. 27 : 1) shows : Quemadmodum audivi a quodam presbytero (later it runs : inquit ille senior) qui audierat ab his qui apostolos viderant et ab his qui didicerant. But Irenæus (v. 36 : 2) refers to the "presbyters" without any additional designation.

NOTE 149, p. 176. — As witness to his existence, Dionysius of Alexandria (232, superintendent of the Alexandrine School of Catechumens) quotes

in Euseb. vii. 25 : 6 the mere fact that there were
two monuments at Ephesus inscribed with the
name of John, and Eusebius busies himself (iii. 29)
more closely with attempting to give more weight
to the testimony of Papias to the existence of the
second John ; in support of which he brings forward, evidently following the lead of Dionysius,
the existence of the two Johannean monuments at
Ephesus.

NOTE 150, p. 180. — In the last passage we
have τὰ λόγια without any further designation ; he
refers however to what goes before, where we
have τῶν κυριακῶν λογίων.

NOTE 151, p. 185. — Eusebius speaks of Papias
even at the time of Trajan.

NOTE 152, p. 187. — The memorandum in a
Latin Oxford codex of the fourteenth century, respecting the four Marys, on whose margin is written the word Papias, is unquestionably to be referred to a Papias of the middle ages, if there is
any meaning to be ascribed to marginal words.
In such excerpts, particularly as they are given in
the Catenas and similar works, the addition of the
author's name is a matter of the greatest untrust-
worthiness.

NOTE 153, p. 189. — So e. g. Zeller : " The si-

lence of Papias will always afford conclusive evidence against the authenticity of the Gospel of
John." Theol. Jahrb. 1847, p. 199. Hilgenfeld:
" Had Papias said the least thing respecting a Gospel of John, Eusebius could not possibly have overlooked it, and as he examined into the works transmitted by John, he could not have kept silence had
there existed a written Gospel from his hand. Die
Evangelien, p. 344. Strauss: "The silence of Papias respecting John as the author of this Gospel is the more weighty in that he not only expressly assures us that he has carefully looked into
what was left behind by John, but that, as the
bishop of Asia Minor and an acquaintance of Polycarp, the disciple of John, he would consequently
know something more definitely respecting the
apostle, who spent his later years in Ephesus."
Leben Jesu, p. 62. Renan: "Papias, qui avait re-
cueilli avec passion les récits oraux de cet Aristion
et de ce Presbyteros Joannes, ne dit pas un mot
d'une Vie de Jésus écrite par Jean. Si une telle
mention se fût trouvée dans son ouvrage, Eusèbe,
qui relève chez lui tout ce qui sert à l'histoire lit-
téraire du siècle apostolique, en eût sans aucun
doute fait la remarque." Vie de Jésus, 3d éd. 1863,
p. xxiv. Volkmar: "We may therefore certainly
presuppose that had Eusebius found a trace of the
use of the anti-chiliastic Gospel of Papias he would
all the more eagerly have brought it out;" and this
opinion is preceded by the remark that "Papias

edited his collection and interpretation of the
Lord's prophecies about the year 167 of our era."
Ursprung uns. Evv. p. 59.

NOTE 154, p. 191. — ʽΟποίαις κέχρηνται τῶν ἀντι-
λεγομένων, τίνα τε περὶ τῶν ἐνδιαθήκων καὶ ὁμολογουμέ-
νων γραφῶν καὶ ὅσα περὶ τῶν μὴ τοιούτων αὐτοῖς εἴρηται.

NOTE 155, p. 192. — That 1 John and 1 Peter can
not be taken out of this category Eusebius himself
declares, vi. 14, when he speaks of Clement. (See
text immediately following.) From the representation of Cosmas Indicopleustes in the seventh
book of his Topographia Christiana we learn in
like manner that the authenticity of all the catholic epistles was contended against.

NOTE 156, p. 196. — The statement of Andrew
in the sixth book that Papias bore witness to the
trustworthiness (τὸ ἀξιόπιστον) of the Apocalypse
neither coincides with the assertion that Eusebius
overlooked the testimony borne to the Johannean
Apocalypse by Papias, nor, still less, with the suspicion uttered by Volkmar (p. 59) that Eusebius
passed over this evidence " on account of his partisan feeling against the Apocalypse." It is decisive against this suspicion that Eusebius has mentioned Justin and Theophilus as credible witnesses
for the Apocalypse.

NOTE 157, p. 197. — Hilgenfeld sought to take away the force of this proof, and wrote in his journal, 1865, pt. 3, p. 335: " Manifestly it is quite a different thing if Eusebius does not hold, in regard to the epistle of Polycarp to the Philippians, the testimony in behalf of the epistle of Paul to this community, an epistle which is unquestionably Pauline in its origin; and merely remarks, though expressly, the use of the first epistle of Peter, which, although a subject of dispute, unquestionably belonged to the much contested catholic epistles." In more prudent fashion, however, Hilgenfeld mentions to his readers the epistle to the Philippians merely, to whom Polycarp himself writes, and does not mention that the extracts are taken from many other Pauline letters.

NOTE 158, p. 195. — As lately as 1865, Hilgenfeld wrote: " How can the inference be drawn otherwise than that Eusebius searched carefully in Papias also for all evidences of New Testament writings, and failed to communicate anything respecting the canonical fourfoldness of the Gospels, and especially respecting the Gospel of John, only because he found no evidence? " " Who does not see that the fourfoldness of the canonical gospels had no existence at the time of Papias? "

NOTE 159, p. 198. — See Volkmar i. a. l. p. 61: " It is an entire distortion of the case for Tischendorf to try to trouble me with the 'absurdity' of the notion that Papias knew nothing of Luke as well : he may just as well have been acquainted with Luke's Gospel as with John's, but may have looked down upon both as too free, Paul-like, anti-Judaic-Christian and anti-chiliastic." " Although he does not defend himself exactly so in respect to the Gospel of Luke, the reason is that it was not enough held in common regard as Luco-Pauline, and he did not need his millenary traditions to defend himself against such a non-authority. What follows, therefore, from this nearer examination of the Papias contexts in relation to the Gospel of the Spirit's Parusia? Either he really did not become acquainted with it in his own Hierapolis, or he did not discover it with the superscription 'according to John,' and certainly not having canonical authority to be disowned by his silence. His testimony remains therefore unchanged ; it must be taken without evasion. Papias's silence respecting Luke and John does not bear direct witness indeed for the non-existence of their Gospels, but for their non-apostolical authority ; or rather that both Gospels were without apostolical authority with the larger number of contemporaries for whom Papias gathered and expounded his chiliastic traditions."

Note 160, p. 199. — During my recent visit to Rome (March, 1866), Cardinal Pitra, the learned Benedictine, called my attention to this manuscript; yet Cardinal Jos. Mar. Thomasius had already given place to the prologue accompanying it in his collections (Opp. omnia, tom. i. Rome, 1747, p. 344), where Dr. Aberle of Tubingen had noticed it, and learnedly discussed it in the first number of his Quarterly, 1864, pp. 1–47.

NOTE 161, p. 200. — It is further stated : Disscripsit vero evangelium dictante Iohanne recte. That the writer of this prologue wanted that this should be understood of John, the prologue prefixed to the Greek Catena text to John, and edited by Corderius, proves, which runs thus: ὑπαγόρευσε (sic)τὸ εὐαγγ. τῷ ἑαυτοῦ μαθητῇ Παπίᾳ εὐβιώτῳ τῷ Ἱεραπολίτῃ. It is clear that this traditional statement is not to be reconciled with Eusebius. Directly subsequently in the prologue it runs: Verum Marcion hereticus cum ab eo (codex abe) fuisset improbatus, eo quod contraria sentiebat, abiectus est a Iohanne. Is vero scripta aut epistolas ad eum pertulerat a fratribus qui in ponto fuerunt. It has already been stated that this tradition respecting Marcion is not an isolated one.

NOTE 162, p. 200. — III. 36 : 1 is Presbyteri; directly after: Dicunt presbyteri apostolorum discipuli; and shortly before, in connection with the account of the reign of a thousand years : Presbyteri qui Johannem discipulum domini viderunt.

NOTE 163, p. 207. — It has had a great many stadia to run through from its ancient use down to the present use by the Romish Church. After going through several hands in the third and fourth centuries, and after repeatedly undergoing revisions in accord with the Greek text, Jerome formed his text from it, not without reference moreover to Greek authorities which were allied to it. The use of the Romish Church gradually made this the Vulgate. It had, however, experienced many modifications, when the Roman Curia, towards the end of the sixteenth century, took advantage of the general diffusion of manuscripts to execute an official revision of the Vulgate, and it is this which now is authorized in the Roman Catholic Church.

NOTE 164, p. 211. — It is an interesting memorial of the negative school of criticism at the present day, that its representatives, in part at least, take particular pleasure in basing their defense upon just those weighty scripture passages respecting whose want of authenticity the criticism which adheres closely to documentary evidence, as gained from the most recent discoveries, leaves no doubt at all. Among such passages may be reckoned the close of Mark's Gospel, the narrative respecting the adulteress in John, and the story of the descent of the angel into the pool of Bethesda in the fourth verse of the fifth chapter of the same Gospel. Certainly there can be no doubt that it

far better subserves the ends opposed to apologet-
ics to leave such apocryphal passages as these in
both the Gospels mentioned, than by their omis-
sion to seem to give advantage to those who claim
the apostolical origin of those Gospels. That that
alliance between legitimism and its most determined opponents repeats itself on a political field,
argues a wicked misunderstanding on the part of
scholars of reputed orthodoxy.

NOTE 165, p. 214. — *Τὰς λοιπὰς γραφὰς* in this
connection must be referred to other New Testament Scriptures. If those of the Old Testament
were meant, the Pauline epistles would here be
clearly placed upon the same footing with the Old
Testament.

NOTE 166, p. 214. — Verse 25, against whose
genuineness most serious objections have long been
expressed, has now in the primitive Codex Sinaiticus the most weighty authority against itself.
(It has been an error that down to this time Cod.
63 has been cited in the same sense.)

NOTE 167, p. 214. — For the purpose of super-
seding Grabe's extremely imperfect edition of
this important work, I have long been making the
requisite preparations in the English and French
libraries. It was my good fortune to discover in

1844 an entirely unknown manuscript bearing on this matter, in the island of Patmos.

NOTE 168, p. 215. — We can understand the remark of I. Nitzsch in 1810 (de Testam. xii. Patriarch. etc. Comm. critica, p. 17), that the author of this Testament could not have lived in the first century, since he alluded to almost all the books of the New Testament. " Si ante casum Hierosolymorum floruisset, hunc non tam diserte indicasset ; sin omnino sæculo primo, non cognovisset ad quos fere omnes allusit Novi Testamenti libros."

For EU product safety concerns, contact us at Calle de José Abascal, 56–1°, 28003 Madrid, Spain or eugpsr@cambridge.org.

www.ingramcontent.com/pod-product-compliance
Ingram Content Group UK Ltd.
Pitfield, Milton Keynes, MK11 3LW, UK
UKHW010347140625
459647UK00010B/880